_____

MY NAME

`T0063138`

_____

TODAY'S DATE

I was given this book because I've:

☐ Decided to follow Christ and live for him.

☐ Got questions about what it means to follow Christ before I make any decision.

☐ Decided to recommit my life to Christ.

☐ Been a Christian but want to better understand what that means.

The best way for you to keep in touch with me is:

_____   _____

PHONE   EMAIL

_____

OTHER

PLEASE RETURN THIS TO YOUR PASTOR OR LEADER OR
WHOEVER GAVE YOU THIS BOOK. THEY OBVIOUSLY CARE
A GREAT DEAL ABOUT YOU AND WANT TO WALK WITH
YOU ON THIS JOURNEY!

IT ALL STARTS HERE

JONATHAN BROOKER

WestBow Press
P R E S S
A DIVISION OF THOMAS NELSON

I'm incredibly grateful for all those who played a part in this book:

God, my Creator, Sustainer, and Inspiration

Dad, for insisting that I use my gifts I've been given and cheering me on along the way

Mom, for always believing in me, listening to me, and encouraging me on my journey

Matthew, Daniel, Jordan, for being not only the best brothers anyone could have but also the best friends

Derek, for designing a beautiful book I'm proud to have my name on

AMPED youth, for allowing me to use you as guinea pigs for this dream

Tidal Wave youth, for allowing me to make all those freshman mistakes in a safe and loving place

Jeanne, for the years of experience you've so lovingly poured into my life as a mentor and second mom

CONTENTS

CONTENTS CONT'D.

HERE'S HOW IT WORKS

This book is for you. It was written to help you. So there's not really a right or wrong way to use it. But since it's here to help you, I want to make sure that it does.

You'll probably want to read a chapter a day. They're relatively short and simple so that you can tackle one piece of the puzzle at a time. You're probably pretty excited right now and may want to read more than one chapter at a time, which is totally ok. But just be careful you don't get going too fast that you're not able to let what you read sink in.

I'll also ask you at times to grab a Bible and read a little more than just a few verses that are already printed here. It's worth doing the extra work of looking them up and reading them! But what if you don't have a Bible? Well, for now you can just look them up on an online Bible site. There are a couple of great ones out there. One of my personal favorites is YouVersion, which can even be downloaded as an app. But you should look to save up a little money and get one you can hold and carry and even mark up, if you want. It's worth it!

Also, you'll see that each chapter ends with a couple of questions to get you thinking and reflecting on what's been talked about. You may not normally journal, but taking a couple of minutes to write down your thoughts helps you to make this stuff personal to you.

And that's important, because this book is for you. Let it help you as you explore and investigate the wonder of what it means to follow Christ!

CHAPTER 01

CAN I GET A DO OVER?

If you're getting this book, chances are you've just recently made the most important decision you could ever make. And it's that choice that we're going to be talking about in more detail as we go through these pages. But it all starts here.

Remember when you were younger and you were playing a game with either your brothers or sisters or with some neighborhood friends? If you were anything like me, there would be certain times that you had perfectly thought through a move or something you were going to do. Maybe it was as simple as you planned to win and then they surprised you and somehow they won. As a young child playing just for fun, I remember countless times when I'd yell out at that point,

"LET'S DO THAT OVER! I WANT A DO-OVER!"

Please tell me you did that once or twice too. I know I'm a competitive person, so I especially like to win, but I don't think any of us likes to lose. So when things had gone wrong, we wanted the chance to do it over.

Ever wish that you could do that in real life?

Wouldn't it be pretty convenient if there were a button you could push like you can on a computer that would just redo, reload, or refresh everything? A fresh start.

That's what happens when you make the decision to give your life to God. You accept the sacrifice that Jesus made for you and allow His Holy Spirit to live inside of you making you new. Some call it being a Christian, which is true, but it's so much more than just a name you wear.

There are plenty of people in our world that wear a name tag that says, "Christian" but have never experienced the abundant life and freedom that are found in letting God give you a fresh start in Him.

It's why the Bible tells us, *"If anyone is in Christ, he is a new creation. The old has passed away; behold, the new has come"* (2 Corinthians 5:17). We're a new creation, a new person, when we're in Christ. That's why I said that this is the most important decision you could ever make. What could possibly be more important than exploring and living out the life you were originally created to live? But that's me getting ahead of myself.

See, I think in some ways the choice you've made to give God your life and accept His gift of salvation is incredibly simple and straightforward. It's why anyone can do it. You don't need to be some college professor, preacher, or perfectionist. It's a message that meets you right at your level. But on the other hand, I know that there are a lot of things you should know about the decision you've made and all that it means for your life from here on...well...to eternity!

As we go through this book, we're going to be answering some of the questions you may have. We're going to try to cover as much of the basics as we can. But you should know that following Jesus thing is something that we get to do all our lives and learn about as we go. So ask questions, even as you're answering the questions that we end each chapter with. Those questions are there to get you thinking, so think. And take a little time to write out your answers and any questions you may have as you go along.

You've just begun the greatest journey of your life. You get the do-over you've always wanted. Congratulations! Your new life has started!

- -

Do-overs aren't really that important if everything has gone perfect and as planned. But life doesn't usually work like that, does it? Why don't you take a minute or two to write down some of the different things that you know you've done wrong. You don't have to be specific. Just list where you could have and should have done something differently.

_____

_____

_____

_____

_____

_____

_____

What does it mean to you, in your words, to be a new creation and get a fresh chance to live life like God planned for you?

_____

_____

_____

_____

_____

_____

_____

If you got the chance to sit across the table from God and look Him in the eye and tell Him what you need from Him, what would you say?

_____

_____

_____

_____

_____

_____

_____

CHAPTER 02

WHERE IT ALL BEGAN

Maybe you've heard the word "gospel" before. It's a word from biblical times where the Greeks used it to say "good news." Now you know why we talk about the gospel of Christ, because what could be better news than this? For the next couple of chapters, we're going to use "GOOD NEWS" to help us discover what this gospel is all about. So for this chapter, we start with where it all began...

<u>G</u>OD CREATED US TO BE IN RELATIONSHIP WITH HIM.

When you read Genesis chapters 1 and 2 (which I encourage you to go do right now!) you'll see that God created the world. Everything in it, even down to separating the land from the ocean, God created it. He just spoke it into existence, and it was there.

In the beginning God created the heavens and the earth. Now the earth was formless and empty, darkness was over the surface of the deep, and the Spirit of God was hovering over the waters. And God said, "Let there be light," and there was light. (Genesis 1:1–3)

That may seem a bit far-fetched and hard to believe. But think of how the president works. If he gives orders to someone or some group of people under his leadership, guess what? They do it. He just says the word, and troops are deployed. He just says the word, and he has a coffee in his hand. His position means that he can just say that he wants something, and for many things, he'll just get them. But the president is just a man. Imagine God, who is above everything, bigger than everything, and perfect. Now if He were to give orders to the world to be created, it would happen. If He commanded the water to separate so some land could come up, it would happen. If He told plants and trees to be there, it would happen. And that's what did happen.

Some say they don't have the faith to believe that. But I think it takes a lot of faith to believe the other option: that stuff was just there and that this world, as incredibly complicated as it is, just happened essentially by accident. You could put a few million monkeys at computers and give them all the time in the world, and they would still never end up writing *Romeo and Juliet*. You could put all the pieces to a Rolex watch in a box and seal it and throw it in the ocean where it would get tossed about for millions of years and it would never ever put itself together to be a working, ticking watch.

Our bodies alone are more complicated than a Shakespeare play or an expensive watch. So how could we possibly believe that this was just by accident? Instead, God tells us that He created us on purpose. And look at that relationship He had with Adam. They were in perfect relationship. Adam and his wife Eve were able to just walk through the perfect garden of Eden with the God that had just spoke the earth into existence. Can you imagine?!

And so the story starts here, and it has to. Without seeing this part of the story, we don't have any real assurance that God wants to even be in relationship with you and me. But look at how He created everything in the beginning. God created man in relationship with Him. And that's the way He wants it.

Some people have this idea that God is some distant, old man in the sky who is like a grandpa sitting on the porch yelling at kids for stepping on his lawn. That picture doesn't really fit with the one that He actually gives us. God shows us that He actually likes taking walks with humanity, talking about life and everything it includes.

This is how it was in the beginning. It was perfect. It was how God intended life to be with Him and us. We need to see this before we get to what happens next.

. . . .

What did God create on each of the days of creation? You can look up the answers in Genesis 1.

DAY 01	
DAY 02	
DAY 03	
DAY 04	
DAY 05	
DAY 06	
DAY 07	

In the last chapter we talked about you being a new creation. Remember that? When you look at how God originally made creation, what does that show you about the relationship that He is looking to get back to with us?

_____

_____

_____

_____

_____

_____

CHAPTER 03

THE DAY EVERYTHING CHANGED

I have a brother that even though he's grown now still cannot really wear a white shirt. As a kid, it didn't take long when he was wearing a white shirt before it would get a stain on it and would no longer be nice and white. Not too much has changed over the years!

And some of you are like that. You have outfits you can't wear because something got dropped, spilled, or rubbed into it and now it's no longer pure and the way it originally was. It's tainted.

As you were told in the last chapter, we're walking through the words "GOOD NEWS" to see what this message of hope is all about. So let's take it to the next step.

GOD CREATED US TO BE IN RELATIONSHIP WITH HIM.
OUR SIN SEPARATED US AND BROKE US.

Like that meatball ruined your favorite shirt, sin came in and ruined the perfect world man was living in. It became tainted.

Grab your Bible and read about it in Genesis 3.

When the woman saw that the fruit of the tree was good for food and pleasing to the eye, and also desirable for gaining wisdom, she took some and ate it. She also gave some to her husband, who was with her, and he ate it. Then the eyes of both of them were opened, and they realized they were naked; so they sewed fig leaves together and made coverings for themselves. (Genesis 3:6–7)

They gave in to the temptation that the serpent, who was the devil, was dishing out. He told them lies and they believed him. God had told them not to eat from a certain tree in the garden and they thought they knew better and did it anyway.

Then everything changed.

Things had been perfect and now they were ruined. And because of that they had to leave the garden and deal with the punishment of sin. Sin, which is when we miss the mark of God's standard for our life, had ruined everything.

If you're like me you may be wondering, "Well why did God even put that tree in there in the first place, then? Or why not keep them from being able to eat it?" If God wanted us people to be in perfect relationship with Him you'd maybe think that He would have kept us from any chance to ruin that. But, if He'd done that – if He'd kept the tree of the knowledge of good and evil out of the garden – then He would have been taking away Adam and Eve's chance to choose whether or not to love and follow Him. Without the tree and the choice, Adam and Eve would have essentially been robots that were forced to love God. And God didn't want robots.

So He created us with what we call a free will. It means that we weren't forced to love God and that we had a choice within His perfect will to decide if we would listen to Him and love Him or if we would ignore Him and do things our own way. So, no, God did NOT create evil. That would be confusing since He looked at His creation and said it was good. But He did create man with a choice. And much like darkness is just the absence of light, evil is the result when good is absent.

It's that sin that is behind the murders, the lies, the stealing, the hurt and pain, and even the tsunamis, tornadoes and earthquakes that have been present throughout history and have even shown up in our lives at times. The broken world we see around us and the brokenness we've experienced within us all goes back to this moment. And now, though Adam and Eve were created perfect, we're all born broken because we're now born with a sinful nature that causes us to sin. It's why, even if you've only ever lied once, you've sinned and nobody needed to teach you how to do that.

Don't you wish you could tell Adam and Eve to take God seriously and not eat the stinkin' fruit?!

. . . .

It's easy for us at times to look at Adam and Eve and think how stupid they were for fall to sin by disobeying God and eating that fruit. But in all fairness, think of a time when you can now see that you did something you knew was wrong and you still foolishly did it. Write a little about it here.

_____

_____

_____

_____

_____

_____

Everything got messed up that day that Adam and Eve sinned. Take a minute to really stretch your imagination and write a little about what in your world today would be different if sin had never entered.

_____

_____

_____

_____

CHAPTER 04

GOOD ISN'T GOOD ENOUGH

Over a hundred years ago a ship sailed out that was on a different level than any other ship that had ever graced the waters of our earth. It was the largest of its kind at the time. And the infamous RMS Titanic was carrying a whopping 2,223 people on April 10, 1912 when it set sail for North America. On this ship there were some of the world's richest people as well as some poor folks who were trying to make a fresh start in America, the land of opportunity.

As you already know, things didn't go as planned. It was only a few days into the trip when the hull of the ship made contact with an iceberg that sent the Titanic on its way to the bottom of the Atlantic Ocean. As it sank, people began piling into lifeboats that would save them from the bone-chilling waters around them. When it was all said and done everyone who had been on that vessel was tallied into two categories that were sent to the New York office and it wasn't rich or poor. It wasn't young or old. It was simply saved or lost.

Let's look at the next part of the "GOOD NEWS."

GOD CREATED US TO BE IN RELATIONSHIP WITH HIM.
OUR SIN SEPARATED US AND BROKE US.
OUR SINS CANNOT BE CURED BY GOOD DEEDS.

We have these ideas of how things should work, even when we're very wrong. It's why some people who will say they don't even believe in God or heaven or hell will say that they believe good people should go to heaven. It's a pretty popular idea. It almost sounds right that good people should go to heaven and bad people should go to hell. The problem is that, as good as this may sound, it's totally wrong.

IT ALL STARTS HERE

If that's how it works then tell me: How good is good enough to be in heaven? Or how bad do I have to be to get sent to hell? How do we measure sin? And how do we ever know if we've done enough good to secure a spot in heaven? That's some shaky ground to be standing on!

But even all those questions, as much as they show the problems with that kind of thinking, don't deal with the biggest problem. And that big problem is that God is perfect. Not just really really really good. Perfect. Absolute perfection. Just so we're clear, that fact is actually really really good. It means that God isn't a bad god. He's an all-knowing, all-loving, perfectly perfect God. But it does mean this…we've got a LOT of space between where we rate and where He is.

God showed us that when He gave His people, the Israelites, the famous 10 Commandments. You may have heard about them before, but take a minute to read the list of what God commands in Exodus 20:1–17.

When you read that list, if you're anything like me, you see at least one thing that you've probably done even though you were told not to, or something you didn't do that you were commanded to do. Yep, we're imperfect people. We've messed up. Some of us in big ways, some of us in only small ways. But the question isn't whether we're bad people or good people any more than the question for the Titanic was whether you were poor or rich.

That list shows us God's perfect standard and that's what much of the Old Testament of the Bible does. And when we see God's perfect standard for how we should live, we eventually realize we can't do it. We mess up. And it's why God tells us that even all the good things we do *are like filthy rags* (Isaiah 64:6). So nothing we could ever do could get God to look at us and go, "Wow there's someone I'm impressed with. They've earned my love!"

All that matters is which category we fall under — saved or lost.

Since you've already talked about the bad things you've done, and we know you're someone who's sinned, why don't you take a little time to write a list of some of the good things you've done!

_____

_____

_____

_____

_____

_____

Now looking at that list above, how do you think you'd rate on a scale of 1–10 - 1 being the worst person alive, 10 being Mother Teresa.

_____

Why do you think we kind of like the idea of being good enough for heaven?

_____

_____

_____

_____

_____

_____

In your own words, why would that idea never work?

_____

_____

_____

_____

_____

_____

CHAPTER 05

TRADING SPACES

The courtroom was stuffy that warm July afternoon as the jury members started filing back in. They had left only a short while earlier and were already back. This was an unsettling sign.

See, the trial had been a brutal one where numerous witnesses had been brought up and a pile of evidence had been given to prove that the defendant was indeed guilty. The prosecution's case was pretty solid. The defense fumbled around at presenting a man of innocence, but it was difficult to prove that kind of thing with how much the evidence proved otherwise. As the jury members took their seats, the question in the mind of the accused man was, "Is there any chance I'm not going to be found guilty and sentenced to death?"

The answer to that question came quickly as the judge called for the verdict and without hesitation the spokeswoman for the jury stared the defendant in the eyes as she coldly declared, "Guilty!"

The police officers made their way to the man to escort him out of the courtroom and towards the electric chair when all of a sudden a man from the back of the room shouted, "Stop! I'll take his spot. You can take me to the electric chair and set him free."

Can you imagine a scene like this? Can you imagine being that man who was sentenced to die and a man you don't even know offers to take your place as someone condemned to die? That would certainly be something!

And it's that something that takes us to our next stop in the "GOOD NEWS."

IT ALL STARTS HERE

GOD CREATED US TO BE IN RELATIONSHIP WITH HIM.
OUR SIN SEPARATED US AND BROKE US.
OUR SINS CANNOT BE CURED BY GOOD DEEDS.
DYING ON THE CROSS, JESUS PAID THE PRICE FOR OUR SINS.

As we already discovered we *"all have sinned and fall short of the glory of God"* (Romans 3:23). And sin cannot be cured by good deeds. The only problem is that if you remember what God said to Adam and Eve in Genesis 3, sin gives us a death sentence. Later in Romans, God tells us that *"the wages of sin is death"* (Romans 6:23).

We were like that man sentenced to die. The evidence was not in our favor, and when the verdict came crashing down it was clear that we were guilty. No good deed or good intentions were going to spare us from our certain death. We can't even argue that it's not what we deserve, because we do. But then, just in the nick of time, someone steps up and takes our place and takes our punishment.

See, Romans 6:23 doesn't just tell us that the cost of our sin is death. Let me show you how the whole verse goes:

For the wages of sin is death, but the gift of God is eternal life in Christ Jesus our Lord.

God gave us an incredible gift through Christ Jesus, and it's life – eternal life. Our sin had given us a death sentence, but God loved us too much to let us carry that weight on our own. So He sent His one and only Son, Jesus, to come and die on a cross in our place to pay the price for our sin, even though He Himself had never sinned. Never.

He came from heaven where everything was perfect. He had the life we all wanted but we didn't deserve. And He came to take the penalty we didn't want but we really deserved. And when He did this He was opening a way for us to spend eternity with Him. So we ended up trading places. He took our spot of penalty so we could experience His spot of eternal glory. Now that is quite a deal, wouldn't you say?!

Going back to the courtroom story, put yourself in the shoes of the convicted man. What would be some of your thoughts when someone shouted out they were taking your place?

_____

_____

_____

_____

_____

_____

Grace is getting goodness we don't deserve. In your own words, why do you think we talk about and sing about "amazing grace"?

_____

_____

_____

_____

_____

_____

Mercy is _not_ getting the punishment we _do_ deserve. Take a minute to just tell God how thankful you are for His mercy and grace.

CHAPTER 06

TURN AROUND!

It may be good, before we keep going on ahead, to take some time to review what we've discovered. We saw that God created the world and humanity in perfect relationship with Himself, and He gave man the gift of a free will. We saw that man abused the free will he was given when he ignored God's instruction and tried things his own way. That messed everything up for everyone because it caused sin to enter into humanity. We found out that since we're now born with a sinful nature, we have a death sentence on our lives. But we also found out some great news! Jesus died on a cross and rose again to pay the price for our sins and give us a chance at a new life!

All this leads us up to our next stop in the "GOOD NEWS."

GOD CREATED US TO BE IN RELATIONSHIP WITH HIM.
OUR SIN SEPARATED US AND BROKE US.
OUR SINS CANNOT BE CURED BY GOOD DEEDS.
DYING ON THE CROSS, JESUS PAID THE PRICE FOR OUR SINS.
NOTICING OUR SITUATION, WE TURN FROM SIN AND TURN TO GOD.

It's so important that we pause to notice our situation because it determines what we should do. It's like noticing that the light turned green and you should go, or noticing that you forgot your wallet and you should go get it before leaving the store with what you were going to buy. When we notice our situation for what it is then we get a better idea of what we should do.

For us, our situation wasn't all that great. We were born with a sinful nature and because of that we've each done our fair share of sinning. Big or small — not like God seems to make the distinction — we have a list of sins we've committed and naturally want to run towards. But look at what God told His people, Israel, to do about these actions:

"Therefore, I will judge each of you, O people of Israel, according to your actions, says the Sovereign Lord. Repent, and turn from your sins. Don't let them destroy you! Put all your rebellion behind you, and find yourselves a new heart and a new spirit. For why should you die, O people of Israel? I don't want you to die, says the Sovereign Lord. Turn back and live!" (Ezekiel 18:30–32)

God doesn't want us to die! Whew! But right here He's giving us some very important instructions on how to make sure that doesn't happen. He uses this meaningful word that you may or may not have heard before: Repent. It means to turn around and go the other way. God is telling His people, which now includes us, that in order to live we need to stop going towards sinful ways that lead to death, repent, turn around, and go towards life.

It reminds me of a true story about a football game that happened way back in 1963. The San Francisco 49ers were playing the Minnesota Vikings. It was the 49ers' ball. Everyone was crunched down. Then the ball was snapped. Everyone was moving when, from out of nowhere, the offense cut through and sacked the 49ers' quarterback which led to a fumble. The ball bounced around for a while and everyone was frantically going for it.

Jim Marshall, a player on the Vikings team, was the one who finally grabbed his arms around the pigskin ball and stood up with it in his possession. He then began to run. As hard as he could, he huffed and puffed his way down the field. His muscles were like fire as he steamed towards the end zone. 20 yards left, 15, 10, 5. Finally he crossed the end zone! The excitement he felt was so overwhelming that he hurled the ball into the stands in celebration.

Then he felt a pat on his back. Someone had joined him in his celebration. He turned around to see it was the offensive tackle, Bruce Bosley, of the other team. Jim Marshall had just ran the ball the whole way down the field in the wrong direction. And instead of making a touchdown he had just made a safety and gave the other team 2 points!

All of this happened because Jim Marshall didn't totally realize the situation he was in. Likewise, it's essential that we realize the situation that we're in so that we can run in the right direction. God has offered us life. He's paved the way. But in order to accept what Jesus did we'll have to turn around, stop running towards our sin, and begin running towards God. Repentance is that critical step in the good news where we use the free will God's given us to choose to run from the destruction of sin and run towards the life in Jesus.

Sometimes we can see sin as fun and enjoyable. That's what makes it so tempting! But from what you've seen so far, how do you think God views it? Maybe you can look at the verses mentioned in this chapter to help you out.

_____

_____

_____

_____

_____

What challenges do you think there might be in repenting and making the turn from sinning to following God?

_____

_____

_____

_____

_____

Turning to life in Jesus is a journey of hope, joy, and peace. So what are some of the things you're hoping God does in your life as you run towards Him?

_____

_____

_____

_____

_____

_____

CHAPTER 07

THE ONLY TRUE WAY

The forest had been on fire for days and it was only spreading and getting worse as it tore through acres of beautiful woods and took houses and buildings that stood in its way without a thought. The dry summer had made it especially dangerous and this fire was taking advantage of all the dry wood that lay on the floor of the forest.

The forest fire was being fought both on the ground with firefighters as well as from helicopters that were dropping water. But then the winds shifted and before long a couple of the firefighters found themselves surrounded by fire and blinded by the smoke. A helicopter flew overhead and dropped a weighted message that they found as it hit the ground near them. It told them that the fire had surrounded them except for a small corridor of forest they could run through to freedom. But they had to move quickly before the time was gone for them to be able to make it through.

The men ended up being saved. How? They followed the instructions they'd gotten from above. They didn't question it, because they knew that they were blinded by the smoke and in need of help and that the message came from above where someone could see everything they couldn't.

And this gets us to our next stop in the "GOOD NEWS."

GOD CREATED US TO BE IN RELATIONSHIP WITH HIM.
OUR SIN SEPARATED US AND BROKE US.
OUR SINS CANNOT BE CURED BY GOOD DEEDS.
DYING ON THE CROSS, JESUS PAID THE PRICE FOR OUR SINS.
NOTICING OUR SITUATION, WE TURN FROM SIN AND TURN TO GOD.
EVERYONE WHO TRUSTS IN JESUS ALONE HAS ETERNAL LIFE.

One day Jesus was talking to his disciples and was telling them about how He was going to die and then raise from the dead and then go to heaven to prepare it for all who would believe in Him. They were incredibly confused by what He was saying and what it meant. One of His disciples, named Thomas, asked Him how they would know the way to where He was going so they could go too. And this was Jesus' answer:

I am the way and the truth and the life. No one comes to the Father except through me. (John 14:6)

Jesus made it clear how His disciples and any of us would get to spend eternity with God. It's only through Him. Like a road that is the only way to get to a house, He is THE way. Like 2+2=4 and not 3, He is THE truth. Like how we need to take air into our lungs to keep alive, He is THE life. Without Him we are lost, confused, and dead. With Him we are found, informed, and fully alive!

Now I know this can get confusing for some people when we start saying that there's only one way to heaven and it HAS to be through Jesus. That sounds so straightforward and we live in a world that likes to think that nothing can be that sure. We also live in a world that has a lot of people trying to say that we should be open to other ideas and ways of living other than just being "narrow-minded" and following Jesus.

But like the men who were surrounded by fire would have burned if they had tried a different way out, we can stubbornly look for other ways to get to heaven when the only Way has been already shown. And if Jesus is a person we can be in relationship with rather than just some theory we believe in, then it makes a lot more sense that we would choose Him and only Him. It's the same reason that you don't look at someone who decides to get married and tell them that they should still explore other options. As ridiculous as that sounds, it's just as ridiculous when someone asks me if I've "tried other religions." Why would I cheat on my love if I've already found the only way to true life?

The harsh reality is that choosing any other way is certain death. That's why this matters so much!

. . . .

What did the firefighters have to do in order to get out? There was an action you should write, but also look at what "E" stands for to help you get a full answer.

Why can we trust God's words about how to get to heaven?

Have a little fun here. What would happen if we had that "that's good for you, but I believe something different" idea with driving directions to somewhere across the country?

CHAPTER 08

WE'RE GONNA LIVE FOREVER

It's hard imagining what forever will be like. Considering how everything around us has a beginning and an end, how do you wrap your mind around the idea of something having a beginning but then going on forever and ever and ever? But that's what God has promised. When we are moved from death to life and are made "new" in Him we get the promise that gets us near the end of "GOOD NEWS":

GOD CREATED US TO BE IN RELATIONSHIP WITH HIM.
OUR SIN SEPARATED US AND BROKE US.
OUR SINS CANNOT BE CURED BY GOOD DEEDS.
DYING ON THE CROSS, JESUS PAID THE PRICE FOR OUR SINS.
NOTICING OUR SITUATION, WE TURN FROM SIN AND TURN TO GOD.
EVERYONE WHO TRUSTS IN JESUS ALONE HAS ETERNAL LIFE.
WITH JESUS, TRUE LIFE STARTS NOW AND LASTS FOREVER.

If Adam and Eve had never sinned – if they'd never eaten of the forbidden fruit – there's every reason to believe they would have gone on living on earth for forever. Obviously that's not how it worked out. But remember how it was sin that caused death? Well, as Jesus makes us right and takes away our sin He offers us this eternal life that is His gift to us. It's His way of righting what has been wronged. The Bible tells us this message all throughout the New Testament: that Jesus is working in and through us to make all things new and right.

That starts now and will last for forever. Take a look at what 1 John 5:11–13 tells us:

And this is the testimony: God has given us eternal life, and this life is in his Son. He who has the Son has life; he who does not have the Son of God does not have life. I write these things to you who believe in the name of the Son of God so that you may know that you have eternal life.

The cool thing about this verse is that it doesn't tell us that we **will** **have** eternal life. Just so we're clear, we **will** *have* eternal life. The Bible tells us that in other places. But what it tells us here is really neat and really important for us to understand: we **HAVE** eternal life. Now. If you've confessed your need for God to forgive your sins and accepted Jesus' sacrifice, and have given Him your life then you have already begun your eternal life.

That means that you've already started building that relationship with the God you're going to get to spend all of eternity with. It means you've already started investing in that eternity. And it means that you can start to experience the benefits of a life that will last forever today. Now.

It's why those first followers of Jesus lived the way they did. (You can read about them and what they did in the book of Acts in the Bible.) They realized their life was grounded in Jesus and, because of that, they would live forever in heaven with Him. So if they had to even give up their life for what they believed then that was really no big deal because they were going somewhere way better.

While Jesus walked the earth and taught people He was constantly warning people that if they tried to hold on to life here too tightly they would lose it. But He also told them that if they lost their life to Him by giving it over to Him then they really weren't losing anything but gaining everything.

So the pay off for giving our lives over to Jesus Christ and putting it back in the hands of the One who created it is that He can bring our dead hearts back to life and this inner life can't be killed. So we get to look forward to an eternity of enjoying God and all that He is!

We often like to hold onto our lives like Jesus said not to. What areas in your life have you been guilty of really holding on to control? These areas will probably be what Jesus points out to you to give over.

_____

_____

_____

_____

How would knowing you have eternal life affect your boldness and confidence here and now?

_____

_____

_____

_____

_____

Who are some people you definitely would like to spend eternity with?

_____

_____

_____

_____

CHAPTER 09

THE SECRET'S OUT

Way to go making it to this point! This is important stuff and you obviously see that. This chapter brings us to the close of the first part of this book where we're trying to get the general idea of what this new life is all about. It's all about the good news. So let's finally take a look at the full breakdown:

GOD CREATED US TO BE IN RELATIONSHIP WITH HIM.
OUR SIN SEPARATED US AND BROKE US.
OUR SINS CANNOT BE CURED BY GOOD DEEDS.
DYING ON THE CROSS, JESUS PAID THE PRICE FOR OUR SINS.
NOTICING OUR SITUATION, WE TURN FROM SIN AND TURN TO GOD.
EVERYONE WHO TRUSTS IN JESUS ALONE HAS ETERNAL LIFE.
WITH JESUS, TRUE LIFE STARTS NOW AND LASTS FOREVER.
SHARING OUR STORY SPREADS THE WORD ON WHAT GOD HAS DONE.

I've had the distinct privilege of standing on top of one of the most active volcanoes in Nicaragua. I'm a pretty adventuresome and, well, crazy person so I absolutely loved it. I imagine some of you would love that kind of opportunity. Well, go on a missions trip and you may get it! But that's not the point I'm trying to make here. So let me get back to it.

That volcano first started before anyone knew about it. As I'm sure you know, there was a lot going on under the surface before anything happened above the surface. But then one day things shifted and BOOM there was clearly a volcano. People would look and could clearly see that it was a volcano.

Likewise, there's something Jesus told His followers to do to show what was going on on the inside. He told them to be baptized. Actually to be fair, Jesus never point-blank told His followers to be baptized (most likely because they already had been). But let's take a look at what His parting words were to His disciples before He ascended back to heaven:

"Therefore go and make disciples of all nations, baptizing them in the name of the Father and of the Son and of the Holy Spirit." (Matthew 28:19)

So, what was the next step after Jesus' disciples or followers went out and got more people to believe in and follow Jesus? Baptize them. So what would be the next step for those people who just put their faith in Jesus? Be baptized.

But why is this baptism thing so important? And is it really essential to being a Christian? Well let's look at it like this: If a man gets married to a woman he will usually have a new piece of jewelry afterwards, right? He's probably now wearing a ring on his left hand on his ring finger. And this ring, whether silver or gold, sends a message to people. That message: "I'm married."

Could someone who isn't married wear a ring on that finger and pretend like they were married? Sure. But they wouldn't actually be married. That's the same way someone can be baptized and go through the motions but not actually have had their life changed by Christ. Now what if a married guy chose not to wear his ring. Would he suddenly be unmarried then? Well, no, he would still be married. But I can imagine his wife would have some real issues with why her husband didn't want to show people he was married. In the same way, you can certainly be a Christian and not have been baptized, but since it shows others around you that you've given your life to God I would wonder why you wouldn't want to do that.

Baptism is a wonderful chance for you to tell the story of what

God's done in your life. It's a picture of what Jesus did for you and what He's done in you. Let me explain.

See, when you go down into the water it's a picture of you being buried; it's a picture of you being dead. Jesus died for our sins and so, in a sense, He took our old selves to the cross so that our new selves could be born. So when you go under the water you're demonstrating the death of your old self. And when you come back up it's a reminder that Jesus didn't just die but that He rose again. And it's a sign that not only did your old self die, but your new self was born in Him. And that's what Paul, a guy who had his life radically changed by Jesus and ended up writing much of the New Testament of the Bible, referred to in Romans 6:2–4:

Since we have died to sin, how can we continue to live in it? Or have you forgotten that when we were joined with Christ Jesus in baptism, we joined him in his death? For we died and were buried with Christ by baptism. And just as Christ was raised from the dead by the glorious power of the Father, now we also may live new lives.

So is the "secret" out in your life yet?

. . . .

Baptism is about us sharing with those closest to us what God has done in our lives. While you've heard it described in other people's words, put what God has personally done for you into a few sentences of your own as if you were explaining it to a friend.

_____

_____

_____

_____

_____

You may have some more questions about baptism. If so, why don't you write them down here.

_____

_____

_____

_____

Now you're ready to talk to a pastor about getting baptized. So don't wait. If they haven't already come to you about it, go to them! I dare you.

Way to go making it to this point! This is important stuff and you obviously see that. This chapter brings us to the close of the first part of this book where we've looked at the good news about our new life in Jesus. But we're not done yet! The rest of this book will be covering a bunch of the basics of what this new life in Jesus is all about. And hopefully it will answer some questions you may have...

CHAPTER 10

NO NEED FOR DUSTY TROPHIES

I don't know too much about dusty trophies, but that's mostly because I don't know too much about trophies. Growing up, I was never too athletic, though I did play soccer for a number of years as a kid. And you know how they are when you're playing sports that young – everyone's a winner! And so I got a few small trophies for...for...well, I'm sure it was for something monumental, of course!

Maybe you've collected some trophies for different accomplishments you've had, as well. They're certainly nice to have around. Depending on how significant of an accomplishment they represent affects how much we probably take care of them and how intentional we are about presenting them. I mean, my trophies are in a box somewhere in my parents' attic, but if I somehow were to have won a Heisman trophy (and this is certainly make believe!) you better believe that beast would be in one of those fancy glass cases with the lights shining on it and everything.

However, all of these trophies – both the highly significant and the "thanks for playing" ones – share some of the same characteristics. They signify something that happened, something that's now in the past. And another common characteristic of all trophies is that they gather dust. They sit and are often untouched, unmoved, and unimportant in everyday life.

Unfortunately, that's how things can become with our relationship with God if we're not careful. Too many people allow their salvation experience to be just like that dusty trophy. Sure, it's highly significant to them, if they were asked. But in all reality it is mostly just something that speaks of an event from the past that has sort of sat on a shelf in their lives being relatively untouched and ignored. Salvation gets treated more like a "get out of hell free" card than an invitation to have an adventurous relationship with our Creator and Savior.

Let's take a look at someone from the Bible who can give us a picture of what it's like to have an active, meaningful, daily relationship with God. David is his name and considering the fact that at one point God says that this guy is a man after His own heart, I'd say he's certainly worth looking at and learning from:

O God, you are my God,
> *earnestly I seek you;*
my soul thirsts for you,
> *my body longs for you,*
in a dry and weary land
> *where there is no water.*
I have seen you in the sanctuary
> *and beheld your power and your glory.*
Because your love is better than life,
> *my lips will glorify you.*
I will praise you as long as I live,
> *and in your name I will lift up my hands.*
My soul will be satisfied as with the richest of foods;
> *with singing lips my mouth will praise you.*
On my bed I remember you;
> *I think of you through the watches of the night.*
Because you are my help,
> *I sing in the shadow of your wings.*
My soul clings to you;
> *your right hand upholds me.* (Psalm 63:1–8)

David paints quite the picture of someone with a real desire for relationship with God. Sure, he'd seen God do cool things in the sanctuary. But David was not satisfied to simply have some amazing church service to look back on. He was hungry and thirsty for more! He was clinging, singing, thinking of, praising, glorifying, longing for, and earnestly seeking more.

When you begin your relationship with God you are beginning something that is a lifelong adventure of more. There will always be more God wants to tell you, more He wants to show you, more He wants to do in you, and more He wants to do through you. We just have to be careful that we don't allow ourselves to get too easily satisfied with *enough*. So go for more than just enough. And don't become one of those people who have their relationship with God sitting on a shelf collecting dust. Instead, spend the time regularly to pursue a deeper relationship with God that affects your life today. After all, that's what He wants!

. . . .

Our relationship with God is different than any other relationship we have, because we can't physically see Him. And yet we can build it a lot like we would other relationships. How do you build a relationship with a close friend?

_____

_____

_____

_____

Why do you think it's a temptation at times to allow our relationship with God to become a dusty trophy that just sits on a shelf?

_____

_____

_____

_____

Take a pointer from David and write your own little note or psalm to God that tells Him what you want from your relationship with Him.

_____

_____

_____

_____

_____

_____

_____

_____

_____

IT ALL STARTS HERE

CHAPTER 11

TALKING TO GOD

Whenever you try something new isn't it nice having someone who can show you "the ropes"? Someone who can explain how it works. You want to try a new hobby and you have a friend who is known for being really into it show you how it works. Whenever we pick up something new it's good to either read up on it and become familiar with it that way or to talk to someone who has some significant expertise or knowledge about whatever it is.

We talked in the last chapter about how important it is that we have an active, daily relationship with God. And as we already know, for any decent relationship to work, there are two basic elements that you have to do: talk and listen. That's pretty simple, right? But it's true. For any relationship, communication is key. But the twelve men who lived alongside Jesus on a daily basis had a question for Him one day: How on earth do you communicate with God in heaven?

They did the smart thing by asking someone experienced in this kind of thing. They asked the only One among them who knew perfectly how to talk with God because He'd come from where He lives. So let's take a look at what Jesus had to say to His followers about how to pray:

"This, then, is how you should pray:

"'Our Father in heaven,
hallowed be your name,
your kingdom come,
your will be done
*   on earth as it is in heaven.*
Give us today our daily bread.

Forgive us our debts,
        as we also have forgiven our debtors.
And lead us not into temptation,
but deliver us from the evil one.' (Matthew 6:9–13)

Just so we're clear, Jesus is NOT telling us that we now have a script we need to follow word-for-word. There is no script for our prayers, just navigation. That means Jesus isn't looking to give us a formula for how we talk to God, just some tips. So let me show you some of the tips you can use in your life as you spend time talking to God:

"Our Father" – Recognize that the One you're talking to isn't some policeman in the sky. He's your Father! When you became new in Him, the Bible tells us that you were then adopted into His family. He chose YOU to be His son or daughter.

"in heaven" – God has the sky high perspective. So when you talk to Him you're talking to the One who sees it all. He sees your life situations and the problems you're talking to Him about in a way that you never will. So you can trust Him to see what you don't because He's in heaven.

"hallowed be your name" – "Hallowed" is probably not a word used very often in your everyday speech, but it means holy or separate because of greatness. So Jesus is saying that when you talk to God that you should worship Him for how great He is while you talk to Him. It can be as simple as "God, you're awesome!"

"your kingdom come, your will be done, on earth as it is in heaven" – It's pretty simple. We can be naturally pretty selfish. We want things to work our way. But when you talk to God and you're telling Him about what's going on in your life and what you want, you need to want one thing more than anything else: God, You do what's best!

"Give us today our daily bread." – Now this is the part we usually jump to

right away. This is where you ask God to provide for the needs you have. Notice that Jesus puts this in after we've recognized who God is, where He is, and admitted that we want His will more than our will. But also make sure you realize that this part of asking God for our needs IS in here. We shouldn't treat God like Santa Claus and just give Him our Christmas list when we talk to Him. But yes, absolutely, you should ask God for things. He is your Father after all!

"Forgive us our debts, as we also have forgiven our debtors." – It's also good for us to make things right with God when we talk to Him. When you get saved you begin to be made like Christ but you don't suddenly become perfect. So what do you do when you mess up? Talk to God about it.

"And lead us not into temptation, but deliver us from the evil one." – This is where you follow up what you just confessed with asking God to keep you from that stuff that tends to hijack your life. We're each wired a little differently in what most tempts us, and so this is where we ask God to help us avoid the particular stuff that can get us off track.

That's where the prayer ends and also where it begins, because this is where your prayer starts...
· ·

If you were talking to God right now, what would you say? Maybe you want to even take the elements of Jesus' prayer and put them in your own words. But this is the only question for today, so take some time on it.

_____

_____

_____

_____

_____

IT ALL STARTS HERE

CHAPTER 12

HEARING FROM GOD

A good relationship is built from good communication. And good communication is built from good talking and good listening. And since we already discussed how we can have good talks with God, let's move on to how we can better hear from God. This is probably one of the biggest questions Christians, especially new Christians, will ask about. How do I hear from God?

But let's ask a question that we need to answer first because it may come up at some point and you may start to really wonder: **Does God even want to say anything to you?** I mean, if we're going to talk about how we can hear from God it's probably good that we start off by settling the fact of whether God wants to say anything to you or not. The good news is that He absolutely does.

One day Jesus was talking to some of His critics and, in the middle of an illustration about how He's a good shepherd to His "sheep" (that's those of us who follow Him), He said this:

My sheep listen to my voice; I know them, and they follow me. (John 10:25)

That means He wants to talk and that also means that He IS talking! So that gets us back to that first question. So how can you hear from God?

Well, there are a few ways that God's given for us to hear from Him. Let's start with the Bible. The Bible is God's written word that He uses to tell us about who He is, how He has worked, what He looks to do in us, through us, and for us, and the future that He has planned. That's a lot! And it's completely reliable (but we'll get to that soon). So this makes the Bible the most dependable way of hearing from God. It's not going to change; it hasn't for thousands of years. And it is on its own level. Check out what the Bible tells us about how it works:

For the word of God is living and active. Sharper than any double-edged sword, it penetrates even to dividing soul and spirit, joints and marrow; it judges the thoughts and attitudes of the heart. (Hebrews 4:12)

The Bible is living and active. How can that be possible? It is, after all, a book. But the fact of the matter is that, speaking from personal experience, it is a book completely unlike any other. I've been reading the Bible since I was a little kid. You'd think I'd be tired of reading it by now. I have some books that I like and will occasionally reread once or twice. But I've read pieces of this one book on a daily basis and have therefore read it through dozens of times in my lifetime so far. And that's just...different.

One of the reasons I can do this and enjoy it so much is because God speaks to me through it! I actually get to hear God using the words of people thousands of years ago to speak to me today. There are times when I read passages of Scripture and I can tell that He's trying to get something across to me. It's why I keep a journal handy whenever I read it, because I can be reading a passage of Scripture that I've read a ton of times and yet He'll say something to me that seems almost new because it's specific to where I'm at right then. And isn't that what you want?

Another way that we get to hear from God is through prayer. Talking to God is only a part of prayer. Can you imagine talking to a friend over coffee or maybe lunch and they spend the entire time doing all the talking and never once ask you what you think? That'd be pretty rude! In the same way, we need to be careful that we do ourselves the favor of making sure we listen to God when we pray.

Up to this point in my life God has yet to speak to me audibly when I pray. But there have been times when a thought will jump into my head while I'm praying that seems to have come from nowhere. And there have been times when it's just been a tug on my heart and my emotions move a certain way. It can be simple, and sometimes it can be a bit more detailed. But if it's in line with what God says in His Word then I take that "random" thought or feeling as a word from God.

Some people may be scared by that kind of thing. "What if it's me?" "What if I misunderstand it." Well, let me remind you that God's sheep recognize His voice. So become familiar with His voice and then learn to trust Him. He's in control. Don't let doubt rob you of God getting to speak to you. After all, it's because of stepping out and trusting God that I knew God was calling me to do full time ministry. So you may not know what God is looking to tell you!

And finally, let me just quickly say that God also speaks through other godly people in your life. So I just mentioned that God spoke to me while I was praying and called me in to full time ministry. It was just a thought, an impression, a feeling that I had when I was at a retreat at the young age of twelve. What was so neat was when God spoke that same message to my youth pastor a few months later and he said he felt that's the direction I was going to go in. I hadn't mentioned anything to him about it and yet God was using him to speak to me. And God will use godly people in your life at times to speak to you. Just make sure that these things always agree with what the Bible already says. That's our way of checking to make sure we're not getting off base.

So we've answered the question of whether God wants to talk to you. We've also answered the question of how we can hear from God? I guess the only question left is one that only you can answer: Will you listen?

Which of the ways of listening to God do you think will be easiest for you? Why?

_____

_____

_____

_____

_____

Which of the ways of listening to God do you think will be hardest for you? Why?

_____

_____

_____

_____

_____

What questions do you have for God to answer in your life?

_____

_____

_____

_____

_____

CHAPTER 13

A BOOK ON ITS OWN SHELF

I want you to imagine something for a moment. I want you to imagine that ten contemporary authors are put in a room and asked to write on one subject. After they're finished then you collect their writings and compare them to each other. If you actually did that, do you think that all of those authors' writings would agree with each other? Nope! You'd have some that were pretty similar, but then you'd have some that were definitely disagreeing with others.

What's crazy is that the Bible was written by over 40 different authors. They came from all different walks of life — a fisherman, a military general, a political leader, a doctor, a king, a rabbi, and a tax collector are just some examples. And yet it all fits together perfectly and has one clear message without disagreements.

Then think of how much time changes things. Have you ever tried to talk to your grandparents about a new gadget you've gotten for your birthday or Christmas? That can be some of the greatest amusement! Decades ago people didn't have cell phones and nowadays you can't walk down a street in America without seeing them being actively used not only to make calls but to do just about everything. So in a world that's constantly changing, imagine something standing the test of time and being important even after many years. The Bible writing spans a time period of about 1,500 years and yet it has one clear message. And, even though the last books were written almost 2,000 years ago, the Bible is still so significant and meaningful to people today that it's impossible to get accurate statistics on how many are sold each year because they're everywhere!

Even the styles of the writing are different at times. You've got history, law, poetry, prophecy, biography and personal letters all included in this one book. How could all these styles mesh together? They do in the Bible!

So the Bible is certainly intriguing. But it's more than just interesting. I said earlier that it is reliable. Allow me to share some things that lead me to believe that that's absolutely true.

I want you to think of the word "never." Never. There has never been a book that has been passed along through time like the Bible. Some people may try to argue that because it's such an ancient book that it can't be trusted. But did you know that throughout history there were groups of people (the Talmudists, the Massoretes, and the scribes) whose only job was to copy the Bible in its exact form. I mean, they had rules that stated that if they made a mistake in their copying that they had to start that page over. They had to always use the original when they started a new copy. They had rules about even what kind of ink and paper to use. Then it just gets crazy. They would count the letters on a given page of the Bible and then, when they finished copying a sheet, they would check to make sure the numbers matched. If they didn't, something must have been wrong, and that sheet got tossed and they started over.

There has NEVER been a book that's been treated this way.

Throughout history, many people have tried to attack this book, but it's made it through. Through the years people have tried to discredit the Bible, but the New Testament has more evidence that it is an accurate reflection of what was initially written than there is for *any* ten pieces of classical literature COMBINED.

All of this is because it was God who worked in the authors to give them the words to say. And He guarded His words through time to make sure that they stayed true. All this because He wanted you to hear that one message that all of the Bible comes together to say:

God so much loved the people that He made, who allowed sin to ruin them, that He Himself came to make a way through His death for us to live free!

The Bible is worth trusting and its message is worth reading over and over and over again.

. . . .

We've talked a lot about the Bible, but now it's your time to dig into one particular verse that talks about the importance of the Bible. So grab your Bible or go online and read 2 Timothy 3:16–17 and use it to answer these questions:

Where did the words of the Bible come from?

_____

_____

_____

What is the Bible useful for?

_____

_____

_____

So why does it matter that the Bible is reliable and so unique?

_____

_____

_____

CHAPTER 14

THAT'S A BIG ELEPHANT

There's this saying that you may or may not have heard before. It goes like this: "What's the best way to eat an elephant? One bite at a time." What it means is that there will be times when the thing in front of you may seem bigger than you can handle but if you simply start "chewing" one bite at a time, then you will eventually accomplish what you'd decided to do.

It's going to work kind of like that when it comes to how you read the Bible. There's no denying that the Bible is a big book and can even at times be a bit confusing. But if you follow some simple helpful tips that we're going to go through and just keep going for it without giving up, then you'll be able to appreciate this gigantically special book for all its worth. This is the book that God uses to shine light on our lives so we can see Him and life more clearly:

Your word is a lamp to my feet
    and a light for my path. (Psalm 119:105)

So first, you need to know that you don't have to read from page 1 to page whatever. The Bible tells the story of God creating mankind and interacting with him, but it's not like other books where you absolutely have to read it straight through. In fact, you may want to jump to the New Testament and read Matthew, Mark, Luke, or John first. Then you get to read about the life of Jesus, the miracles He did, and His death and resurrection for you! It's totally ok for you to start there in the middle of the book. It's not cheating!

Second, read with purpose. This kind of goes with the last tip. Do yourself a favor and don't just flip to any place in the Bible and read a few random verses. Doing that is kind of like flipping through a letter from a significant other and only reading a few lines from it that may be totally out of context. Your best bet is to pick one book of the Bible and start at the beginning and read it through. In fact, you may even choose to read some of the shorter ones straight through all at once and get the full picture of what that book is about. What I usually like to do is to read a chapter at a time and see what God has to tell me in that one chapter, and then the next day I move to the next chapter.

And that leads us to the next tip. Read with reflection. Like we've already said, God is looking to speak to you through His word. If I have someone very important talking to me I will sometimes take notes about what they say. I don't want to miss anything they say and I definitely don't want to forget anything important they've told me. It's kind of the same way with the Bible. Journaling and reflecting on what you read allows you to engage the words your reading. Otherwise you can just read a number of verses and walk away almost forgetting what you'd read. I find that if I can write down just a few things that stood out to me or even some questions I may have, that it helps me significantly in paying attention and allowing God's word to change me.

I want to end by giving you a few more quick "pointers" when it comes to making the most of reading the Bible. Mix it up every once in a while. Read a different translation of a passage you're reading. Sometimes it helps you to understand what the passage is really saying when you read it aloud. Sometimes I like to take the promises of the Bible and "personalize it" by putting my name in where it makes sense. You can also read the same chapters and verses that your friend is reading and talk about what you read and what stood out to you.

All of these ideas are simply ways to take bites. Sure reading the Bible may seem like a big elephant. But as that silly old saying goes, just pull out the fork and knife and start going at it one bite at a time.

Time to put it to practice! So what book of the Bible are you going to start reading? It's ok to ask a leader you respect for help with this.

Now take a minute and read one of my favorite passages: Ephesians 2:1–10

After you've read it once through, read it again aloud.

Now jot down some things that stood out to you.

_____

_____

_____

_____

_____

_____

Let's personalize the message of verse 10 for you. So take "we are" and replace it with your name is, and change "us" into either "him" or "her" and write it out here.

_____

_____

_____

_____

CHAPTER 15

HIDE SO YOU DON'T HAVE TO SEEK

A couple of chapters back I shared about my one brother, so let me share a little about another brother of mine. This one has some interesting quirks and tendencies. In fact, he knows all about them and truthfully, he kind of likes them. One in particular that's always been pretty peculiar is his need to take all the gifts he gets on Christmas morning and sneak them away to his room as soon as he can that same day. They barely make it to lunch before he's stashing them any way he can to sneak them back to his hideaway. I guess it became a habit because he wanted to use them right away rather than just having them sit under the tree, and that he probably didn't want to risk them being lost or taken.

That's why any of us hide things, right? Even the dog who takes his bone and buries it in the back yard wants to use that bone when he wants and does not want somebody or something taking it from him! So he hides it.

David, a guy we talked about earlier, was a man during biblical times who decided that he didn't want anyone taking one of his most precious possessions from him. So what did he do? He hid it...in his heart.

I have hidden your word in my heart
that I might not sin against you. (Psalm 119:11)

For him the word of God was so valuable that he wanted to be able to use it right away rather than just having it "sit around," and he didn't want to risk it being lost in the shuffle of life. I'm not talking about the actual pages of the Bible. I don't think David was as concerned about losing the pages of the Scripture as he was wanting to make sure he didn't lose the message of the Scriptures.

That's why he said he hid the word of God in his heart, so that he wouldn't end up sinning against God. See, when we are far from God's word we're much more likely to be far from God. Hearing from Him helps keep us close to Him. So how do we hide God's word in our hearts? Beyond simply reading it on a daily basis (which I really hope you begin to do!), the two best ways to hide God's word in the back room of our hearts is to meditate and memorize.

Meditation. That word might make you think of some weird Middle Eastern religion where you sit on the floor with your legs crossed, eyes closed, humming, with your hands in some weird formation on your legs. The good news is that that is NOT what I'm talking about. That's actually not what the word even means. What it actually means is extended thought or reflection, contemplation. It's the opposite of speed-reading.

If you wanted to read for completion rather than comprehension, you could probably read through the Bible in a breeze. But sometimes it's good to really take it slow and chew on it. It's like the difference between a microwave dinner and a home-cooked crockpot masterpiece. Sure, sometimes the microwave works, but there should be times when we let the word of God "simmer" inside our souls. Then we can ask all kinds of questions about what we're reading. What does this show me about the character of God? What does this show me about how God interacts with us people? What should I know because of what this says? What should I do because of what this says?

Memorization. You should learn to memorize Scripture and hide it in your heart that way. Why do I think it's so important? Because when you're tempted you can right then and there say, *"No temptation has seized you except what is common to man. And God is faithful; he will not let you be tempted beyond what you can bear. But when you are tempted, he will also provide a way out so that you can stand up under it"* (1 Corinthians 10:13). When you worry you can instantly remind yourself that God says to *"Cast all your anxiety on him because he* cares for you" (1 Peter 5:7). Or when you're feeling beaten up about mistakes you've made and you're feeling unforgiven you remind yourself that God says *"If we confess our sins, he is faithful and just and will forgive us our sins and purify us from all unrighteousness."* (1 John 1:9). Now can you see why it's so good to have these verses hidden away in your mind and heart?

. . . .

In a minute we're going to try this meditation thing out, but before we do I want you to honestly answer this question: What do you think will make meditation and/or memorization a challenge for you personally at times?

_____

_____

_____

Ok, grab your Bible and look at 1 John 3:16. It's near the end of the whole Bible. Read it slowly through.

Now answer those questions I gave you before. (1) What does this show you about the character of God? (2) What does this show you about how God interacts with His people? (3) What should you know because of what you've read? (4) What should you do because of what you've read?

_____

_____

_____

_____

_____

_____

Memorization isn't easy for everybody, and it's something you get better at as you do it more. So why don't you just try one short verse a week. You may want to write it down on a notecard where you can carry it with you or see it often. Here are some verses to consider:

Psalm 119:11

Matthew 22:37

Proverbs 3:5

John 15:5

Titus 3:5

Psalm 103:2

Psalm 103:2

Ephesians 2:8

2 Peter 3:9

Psalm 37:4

Isaiah 55:8

Matthew 11:28

Matthew 6:33

Proverbs 3:6

Jeremiah 29:11

Jeremiah 32:27

John 3:16

Ephesians 2:10

2 Corinthians 5:17

Philippians 4:4

Proverbs 16:3

CHAPTER 16

I NEED YOU

A number of years back my family went on one of those great family vacations, and with my family I'm not being sarcastic about that at all. We have a great time! We happened to be in one of my favorite places on earth, the Smoky Mountains of Tennessee, and we had found a deep creek with waterfalls and a big cliff that you could jump off of into the water. It wasn't too long before my brothers and I, along with my dad, had gone a few rounds of climbing the cliffs only to jump down into the clear water below. My mom, however, was sold on just being a spectator.

When we first asked her to have a try at it she said, "No way!" But we persistently kept hassling her about how she just had to try it at least once since it was so much fun. We knew that she'd actually really enjoy it if only she could get past her initial fears. And we even had some help from a girl who was probably only five years old and who, after a few minutes on the edge of the cliff talking to my mom, went soaring off with a happy scream.

Then there was this woman on the other end of the spectrum who I'm going to guess was in her sixties, though it's hard to say for sure since she was clearly extra aged by her smoking habit. How do I know? Well, when she went to show my mom how she really didn't have to be afraid and could do it, she jumped off the cliff herself — with the cigarette she'd been smoking still in her hand! Eventually my mom did muster up the courage and took the leap off the edge. It was a great moment.

There's something about having other people around us that affects the kind of people we are and what we choose to do. My mom chose to jump because we talked her into it. There was no way she would have just done it. And maybe you've made some bad decisions in your life because you were talked into it by some friends. Maybe you've made some good decisions because of positive influences you've had in your life. I think my mom is still trying to decide which category that day falls under!

God knows the power of people. That's why He put us together into this thing He calls His Church. Church isn't about a building or about pews and services. It's about people. People who aren't perfect but are seeking to be more like Jesus every day — together. Please, hear me and believe me when I say: You cannot do this following Jesus thing on your own.

It's why God was so clear in Hebrews 10:24–25 when He said:

And let us consider how we may spur one another on toward love and good deeds. Let us not give up meeting together, as some are in the habit of doing, but let us encourage one another—and all the more as you see the Day approaching.

Some Christians are in the habit of thinking they can do it on their own and are choosing not to meet regularly with other believers, just like the verse says. They're wrong. Flat out wrong. We need each other! You need your church. It's where you can be encouraged by other people who share a love for the Lord. It's also where you can be an encouragement to others when they need it. It's where you can be taught more about God and how to live your life for Him. It's where you can experience worship in different ways than what you already will have at home by yourself. It's where you can give to the work that God is doing in your community through your church. It's where the life we live is rejuvenated and realigned if it's gotten off track.

No church is perfect, but not being a part of a church is perfectly crazy if you're actually hoping to be all God has created you to be. God tells us that together we form His body that shows the world who He is. So some of us are hands, some are feet, some are eyes, some are ears. We're all different but we're all important. That means you — YOU — are a part of this body that is needed for us to be the Church He wants us to be. So I need you. Don't rob God's church of the gift that is you!

. . . .

What's something positive that you did mostly because you had people encouraging you to do it?

_____

_____

_____

_____

What are some reasons people don't go to church? And, considering what God tells us to do, is there a valid reason for choosing to not do "the church thing"?

_____

_____

_____

_____

It's important to know that no church is perfect because then we don't have to waste time looking for one that is. But thinking of how Jesus loves you, how do you think we should handle problems in our church?

_____

_____

_____

CHAPTER 17

IF YOU REALLY LOVE ME

Have you ever loved something? I'm sure you have. That's a silly question to ask. But I mean, have you ever really loved something? Maybe it was actually a someone and you know you loved them because you thought about them all the time, gave them nice things, and even sacrificed time or money to be with them. Maybe it was something and you invested time, money, thought, and energy into it.

I have one friend who is a pretty die-hard Philadelphia sports fan. He has the jerseys, goes to the games, knows the players, and even knows their stats. I also have a friend who loves a certain type of music so much that he knows more about certain bands than I think the bands themselves even know. As a drummer, he also works tirelessly to figure out the drum parts exactly as they're done on the album. And as complicated as they are, he can actually do it! It's pretty clear what these guys love because their time, their energy, their talk, and their thoughts are all spent on what holds their affection.

The neat thing about our love for *someone*'s rather than *something*'s is that *someone*'s can actually love back. It's a totally different ball game loving someone who can spend their time, energy, talk, and thoughts back on you, rather than a hobby or object that can't. That's what makes relationships so powerful. And that is exactly what makes worship so powerful. Worship is basically our showing our love for God through our time, our energy, our talk, and our thoughts.

More than anything else you could love and go absolutely crazy about, none of them will ever be able to love you back like God can. It's one of the reasons I personally love to worship Him. Because as much as I may tell Him that I love Him and show it through what I'm saying or doing, He

IT ALL STARTS HERE

loves me back more. God loves it when we put Him first in that way, and He responds to it. In fact, listen to what Jesus had to say to a Samaritan woman He was once talking with:

Yet a time is coming and has now come when the true worshipers will worship the Father in spirit and truth, for they are the kind of worshipers the Father seeks. (John 4:23)

See, the woman had been having a bit of a debate with Jesus about how her Samaritan culture and His Jewish culture viewed worship differently. But she was getting it all wrong. She was caught up in the details about place and form. (Read the full story in John 4:1–42).

We can still get caught up about that nowadays. It's why some people feel you can only worship with hymns. It's also why some people feel it's practically impossible to worship with hymns in this day and age. But I think Jesus would say they're both wrong. It's not about the style of music and not about whether we're worshipping in a "real" church or in a room above a bar (yeah, I've actually done that!). It's less about style and location and it's more about spirit and truth.

The spirit is the heart and mind behind what we do. It's what we think about and what gets our energy. God wants us to be passionate about Him, and honestly He deserves it! It's by worshipping God in spirit that you can find your heart and mind soaring as they get lost in the wonder of God and what He's done for you.

If worshipping God in spirit is soaring then worshipping God in truth is the ground that we can firmly land on. It's the logic behind the emotion. See, God doesn't want our worship of Him to be all goosebumps and feelings. He also wants us to spend time with Him, learning about Him, discovering the truth about Him and the truth that is in Him. Just like you will study up on the hobbies or people you're interested in, when you spend time studying up on God you are actually worshipping Him.

So worship, the way we show God we love Him, has two sides. The first is that spirit part where we use the emotions that God Himself gave us to express our love for Him. Some people don't like this because it feels all "mushy gushy." But when you truly realize what God has done for you by giving all of Himself, then you realize it's not cheesy to love Him with all you have. In fact, that just makes sense. And it also makes sense that we love God with truth as well. Just like emotions have their place and shouldn't be ignored, neither should our discovery of more and more of who God is. Both are important parts. Ignoring the emotions may leave you with truth but it's dead truth. And ignoring the truth may leave you with goosebumps but it's just empty hype.

So if you really love God you'll choose to worship Him with all you have — through your time, your energy, your talk, and your thoughts. And you know what's cool? Go look back at John 4:23, because if you worship God in that way then *He's* the one who will seek *you* out! Tell me that's not cool!

· ·

Who or what would your closest friends say you totally love? How can they tell?

_____

_____

_____

_____

_____

_____

_____

_____

We're all wired differently and we'll usually tend to naturally lean towards either the emotional stuff or the intellectual stuff. So which do you tend to go for? And why is it important that you also worship God in the way that's maybe not so natural for you?

We didn't really touch on it, but music plays a big role in worship because it's intensely powerful in teaching us things while at the same time tugging on our emotions. So think of a worship song you really love and write its title and then what it teaches you about God. Then go listen to it and have some time loving on God. If you don't know any, go look for one you can get into.

CHAPTER 18

THE SECOND IS LIKE THE FIRST

Have you ever watched one of those game shows where the contestant has the opportunity at various levels to call it quits and take what they've won so far and call it a day or try for more? I'm sure you have. And so I'm sure you know the catch with a lot of those game shows. The catch is that, if you continue to risk it, you can get to a point where you get a question wrong and you lose it all. It's so painful when I watch someone lose a few thousand dollars because they kept wanting to risk it. Can you imagine being that person? Can you imagine being so close to having so much only to lose it all in the end?

That's a good picture of how our relationship with God can be if we're not careful. Sometimes we can focus on loving God and get so far only to lose it all by getting that last question wrong: How do we love the people around us?

It may seem crazy – but God is very clear that the question of how we love the people around us – even the annoying, rude, or sinful ones – is just as important as how we love Him. How you love your creepy neighbor is as important as how you love God. How you love your annoying sibling who is constantly pushing your buttons is as important as how you love God. Even how you love the strangers that you pass by on any given day is as important as how you love God. You can try to love God well, but if you don't get this loving others thing right then you lose it all.

Just look at what God said about how His love should affect us.

We love because he first loved us. If anyone says, "I love God," yet hates his brother, he is a liar. For anyone who does not love his brother,

IT ALL STARTS HERE

whom he has seen, cannot love God, whom he has not seen. And he has given us this command: Whoever loves God must also love his brother. (1 John 4:19–21)

Even Jesus Himself, when some people were trying to test Him, made sure that He made it clear that loving others is just like loving God.

Hearing that Jesus had silenced the Sadducees, the Pharisees got together. One of them, an expert in the law, tested him with this question: "Teacher, which is the greatest commandment in the Law?" Jesus replied: "'Love the Lord your God with all your heart and with all your soul and with all your mind.' This is the first and greatest commandment. And the second is like it: 'Love your neighbor as yourself.' All the Law and the Prophets hang on these two commandments." (Matthew 22:34–40)

It can be hard to imagine how we could love some people. There are just some people that are easy to love and then there are some others that seem to be nearly impossible to love. We all have them. Loving others would probably be a lot easier if it just weren't for those people. But think of it like this, how lovable do you think you were and are to God? I mean, really, you're pretty great. We all know that. But compared to God you're pretty awful. We all are. There's not a single one of us that really made it easy for God to love us. We disobeyed Him, and sometimes still do. We have issues. We're selfish and we're needy. But you know what's cool? God still loves us.

It's that very fact that allows us to love others. God first loved us. That's what those verses just said. So that's where the love starts. I can love people that are difficult to love because I know that God first loved me and I have His undeserved love living inside of me. If you don't have God's love inside of you then I don't know how you'd be able to love everyone. But if you do have God's love really dwelling in you then I don't know how you could choose not to love everyone.

This is probably one of the simplest ideas but one of the most challenging ones at the same time. But the more we continue to show love to people, even when they don't "deserve" it or can't do anything to repay us, the more we show that God's love really has changed us and that we really do love Him back.

· ·

Let's get right down to it...who would you say is one specific person (or maybe a few) that is especially difficult to love? Why?

_____

_____

_____

_____

What would be the problem if God had waited for you to earn His love?

_____

_____

_____

_____

So what is something specific you can do to show that person love like God showed you? Be specific and avoid saying something that you won't do such as yelling, being mean, etc. Showing love isn't a matter of simply not being mean, it's actively loving someone.

_____

_____

_____

_____

CHAPTER 19

PUT YOUR MONEY WHERE YOUR HEART IS

I have a confession to make. Right now as I'm writing these words for you to read I am multi-tasking and buying some new music. For those who know me best that is anything but a surprise. See, I've always loved music. A lot. I have tens of thousands of songs on my iTunes, stacks upon stacks of CDs, even a record player and a few records that I've bought over the years. I have no idea how much money I've spent over the years to get all the music I have, but I can guess it's probably a pretty hefty amount! That's what we do when we love something, right? We spend money on it.

Can you think of what it is for you? Maybe it's music too. Maybe it's your car. Maybe it's sports gear. Maybe it's your movie collection. Maybe it's books. Maybe it's your video game collection. Maybe it's your wardrobe. I hear teens tell me all the time how broke they are, but I can still tell what they care about – what they love – by what they spend whatever money they do have on.

And that brings us back to the last chapter where we talked about ways we show God our love for Him. There's one way that I held off on mentioning because I wanted to spend this whole chapter on it, and it's what we call tithing. That term may be totally foreign to you, so let me explain it. It literally means *"a tenth"* and refers to ten percent of what we get from our work. In fact, let's take a look at an Old Testament verse where God tells His people about how this tithe thing works.

A tithe of everything from the land, whether grain from the soil or fruit from the trees, belongs to the Lord; it is holy to the Lord. (Leviticus 27:30)

First things first, I'm willing to bet there's a good chance that you are not a farmer. So does this affect you in your life if you're not getting grain from the soil or fruit from the trees? And if so, how? Absolutely it does. And the reason is because God isn't trying to just get some grain or some fruit, He's trying to get your heart.

Let me explain. When this verse was first written most people were farmers and relied on the ground to produce their food and their income. If it was a good year then they had plenty of food and plenty of income. But if it was a bad year, well, you can figure that out. So that's why it matters so much what God is saying here, because He didn't specify if it was a good year or not. He simply said this: "Hey you, one-tenth of whatever you get is not yours. It's mine."

Sounds kind of demanding. It's not even like He's saying that He wants us to give Him a tenth of what we get. He's saying that it already belongs to Him. So that means something pretty serious. It means that, if we are following God and we make $10 doing some chore or something, $9 of that is ours but $1 is already claimed by God. It's already holy, which means set aside. And so that means if we keep all $10 for ourselves and spend it how we want then we...well, we've stolen from God. And that is why I think this matters so much. I don't think we want to be stealing from God!

Some think that this was just something for the Old Testament time. You see, some of the law that we can read in Leviticus was made complete and no longer necessary when Jesus came and died for us. In that moment the rules changed, but not all of them. And this is one that stuck. Just look at what He said when He was correcting the self-righteous Pharisees:

"What sorrow awaits you teachers of religious law and you Pharisees. Hypocrites! For you are careful to tithe even the tiniest income from your herb gardens, but you ignore the more important aspects of the law—justice, mercy, and faith. You should tithe, yes, but do not neglect

the more important things." (Matthew 23:23, NLT)

The Pharisees were following with crazy obedience part of the law but totally ignoring the heart of God for the actual needy and hurting. When you give your tithe to the church it is going towards helping the needy both in your community as well as around the world. But these religious leaders were willing to give to that but then totally ignored justice, mercy, and faith everywhere else in their life. They treated their tithe like they were paying off God. Jesus clears it up by saying that's not how it works. We should tithe AND be people of justice, mercy, and faith.

All this is possible and all of this giving is fueled by that thing we talked about in the last chapter — worship. We should give that first ten percent that is God's not because we feel obligated or because we just think it's a good idea. We should give because, just like anything else in our life, we show our love and affection by how we spend our money. If you don't love God then why give Him money to try to pay Him off? But if you do love God then why would you hold back from Him what is already His that He's given to you as an opportunity to worship?

. . . .

God cares a lot about how we spend our money and how much we care about it. You'll find all kinds of verses about this topic. Judging from your experience, why do you think God would care so much about this?

_____

_____

_____

_____

_____

_____

What do you think would be the biggest challenge in tithing for you? Why?

_____

_____

_____

If tithing is new to you and the way you spend your money (no matter how little you may get in a week's time!) then it probably will mean that you'll have to sacrifice something to be obedient. So take a minute and think, what would you sacrifice? And why would it be worth it?

_____

_____

_____

_____

_____

_____

CHAPTER 20

NEVER EVER FORGET

It was a night much like any other that the disciples had spent with Jesus. The only thing that would have seemed a little special about that night was that it was the Passover. This was a special feast for Jesus and the disciples because they were Jewish in background and this meal held some real significance for them. It dated all the way back to around 1445 B.C. It all started when God was freeing His people (the Israelites) from their slavery to the Egyptians. The pharaoh wouldn't give in and let the hundreds of thousands of free laborers go out and be free. However, the pharaoh wasn't the one in control in this situation; God was.

Take a minute to open up your Bible and read Exodus 12:21–30. Go ahead. We can wait here. It'll explain to you where the Passover comes from and then ultimately where communion comes from.

So let's fast forward back to that night when Jesus was with His disciples in an upper room of some stranger's house. The disciples didn't understand the significance of what was happening that night but Jesus knew that He was soon going to be arrested, unfairly tried in a mock court, and then sentenced to die on a cross. Jesus was about to be sacrificed for everyone's sins so they could be spared. Are you starting to see it?

Jesus was about to be the ultimate sacrificial lamb. That's why you'll sometimes hear Him referred to as the "Lamb of God" – pretty strange otherwise, right?! But Jesus was about to spill His own perfect and sinless blood so that we could have a chance to be spared from our own eternal death in hell. It's heavy stuff, but that's why communion is such an important thing in the church world. Just look at what Jesus said to His disciples that night when He began this ordinance:

And he took bread, gave thanks and broke it, and gave it to them, saying, "This is my body given for you; do this in remembrance of me."

In the same way, after the supper he took the cup, saying, "This cup is the new covenant in my blood, which is poured out for you. (Luke 22:19–20)

"Do this in remembrance of me." Those words have been the church's instructions for almost two thousand years. We have been told we need to remember Jesus and what He did in this way.

I tend to be a pretty forgetful person. It's embarrassing really. All my life I've had issues with totally forgetting people's names, what I was supposed to do, where I'd left something, and so much more. At times I've actually wondered if my mom neglected to tell me that she dropped me on my head or that as a toddler I'd gotten into some paint chips or something. But we can all be pretty forgetful at times. I'm sure you've had times when you forgot something, even something pretty important. All of a sudden you have that moment. You know that moment. It's the one where you freeze and your heart seems to skip a beat because it suddenly occurs to you...you forgot.

No matter how important something is, we can run the risk of forgetting about it or perhaps just forgetting how significant it is. Either way, we can't afford to forget or lose the significance of what Jesus did for us. It should have been my blood that paid for my sins. The same with you. But instead Jesus let His body be broken and His blood be spilt, even though He'd never sinned and was perfect, so that we didn't have to pay for our own sins.

So when we take communion we remember the amazing exchange that was made. We eat the bread reflecting on how the Roman soldiers' whips beat against Jesus' body beating Him to the point where the Bible tells us you could barely tell He was even a person. His body was broken so that you and I could be made whole. We drink the juice or wine remembering that the nails pierced Jesus' hands and feet and that His blood poured out onto that wooden cross for us. His blood was poured out to show us how God's grace was being poured out to you and I. God was fixing our broken relationship with Him.

That's something we can't afford to forget!

. . . .

Take a minute and write in your own words what Jesus' sacrifice means to you. What does it mean to you to have your sins paid for? How does the cross change your life?

_____

_____

_____

_____

_____

_____

_____

What could be some of the dangers of forgetting what Jesus did for you? List as many as you can think of.

_____

_____

_____

_____

_____

CHAPTER 21

THE HOLY SPIRIT

This whole book is about letting you understand what it means to be made new in Christ and then teaching you the basics of what the Bible tells us about God and how we interact with Him. Just so we're clear, let me say again that this is only the start. We all have the exciting task of learning more and more about God until the day we finally get to meet Him face to face in heaven.

But one of the probably more confusing parts of our theology is the Trinity. Now don't get scared by the word *theology*. Theology is simply the beliefs we have about God, and honestly, we all have them. It's just a matter of how true and accurate they are. But anyhow, back to the Trinity. The Trinity is the term we use to describe the fact that God is one God. You've got to make sure you understand that. We don't believe in many gods or even multiple gods. God is one God but He exists in three persons, and that's what we call the Trinity.

Let me give you a metaphor to hopefully help this make a little more sense. Think of an egg. It can be big or small and white or brown - doesn't matter, it's your imagination. Ok, now this egg that you're imagining is one egg. You could hold it, throw it up and down, and pass it around and it would still be one egg. Now if you chose to crack that egg into a frying pan you would put the shell on the counter and maybe separate the yolk (if you're looking to eat a little healthier) and then fry up those yummy egg whites. That one egg has those three parts that are uniquely definable but are still collectively very much...egg. Now that's just a metaphor which means it's a picture of what we're talking about and not exactly what we're talking about. But hopefully this picture helps you to understand this great aspect of the God we serve.

God the Father is our Heavenly Father who spoke creation into existence. Jesus and the Holy Spirit were there too. Just check out Genesis 1:26 and how He says about creating man *"in our image."* As I imagine you already know, Jesus made His big entrance to human history when He came as a little baby in a Bethlehem manger. You remember it because every year you get His birthday gifts under a pine tree. In that moment the world changed because God came and lived among us in the flesh. It was a big deal! The main purpose in His coming and living among us was that He could show us the Father and then that He could die for us and pay the price for our sin that we could never pay. But Jesus said something crazy at one point when He was talking to His disciples. Just look at it:

"But I tell you the truth: It is for your good that I am going away. Unless I go away, the Counselor will not come to you; but if I go, I will send him to you." (John 16:7)

The reason I find this statement to be a bit crazy is because when I think of what it must have been like to have walked and talked with Jesus I can't imagine much better. Sometimes when we're bored my friends and I will ask the question of "if you could go back in time and spend a day with anyone from history who would it be?" and we always have to put the tag on it "except for Jesus, of course." But then Jesus tells His best friends that it was best that He leave so that we would have better than God among us. When Jesus ascended back to heaven, God sent His Holy Spirit and at that point He made it possible for us to have God within us. Now doesn't that sound better?!

The Holy Spirit has come to dwell in you, so that God could make His home in your soul and be the guide to your life. You're no longer alone. The Holy Spirit has come to cleanse you, so that your conscience can be cleaned from within. He also convicts us so that we know when we're about to or have just done something that is outside of or against the perfect plan that God has for us. The Holy Spirit has come to show us

God by allowing us to experience Him within our very lives. The Bible is clear that the Holy Spirit is within us so that as we read the Bible and experience life we will see our Heavenly Father in ways we never could without Him. And the Holy Spirit has come to give us power. Think about it. How could the infinite, immeasurable, unbeatable God inhabit our lives and not bring at least some of that supernatural power with Him? Now we may not always live in that power but it doesn't mean it's not accessible to us.

This is the promised Holy Spirit that Jesus spoke of Who comes to make His home in us when we invite God to become Lord of our lives. And our lives are forever changed because God is doing something — something inside of us.

• •

Look up John 14:23–26 and list as many truths or facts about the Holy Spirit as you can find.

_____

_____

_____

_____

_____

Read Acts 1:8. What seems to be a result of having been given the Holy Spirit? And what have you witnessed God doing in your life or around you?

_____

_____

_____

_____

CHAPTER 22

FIRE-PROOF FAITH

The sun rose in the Middle Eastern sky as a new day started in a strange world for these three young men. Not long ago, they and their people had been in battle against the Babylonians. A battle they lost. As a result of that loss Shadrach, Meshach and Abednego were among a number of young men who were separated from their families as they were carried off to a foreign land to serve, work, and become a regular part of this new society. One of the biggest problems these guys were having with doing that was how different their view of God was from the gods of the people of Babylon. That's what made this day one that would be talked about for hundreds and thousands of years to come.

The king had gone too far this time. The king loved his idols and he believed there were many little gods that made the world work. But a while back he'd decided to make a big deal out of one of those little gods. He ordered that his people make a statue of gold. But this was not a nine inch statue, not a nine foot statue. This was a ninety foot tall nine foot wide, gold statue to honor one of his gods. Can you imagine how much gold that must have taken to make?

Well the king wasn't done at just having a ridiculously huge and expensive statue made. No, he had to go ahead and take it a step further. He made a decree that was passed on by his leadership to the people. And this was the rule: when they started playing the music the people needed to bow down and start worshipping this idol. Sounds pretty ridiculous and pretty silly. So let's say you decided you were too cool to bow down to some little (errr...huge) idol. What would happen? Well the king made it clear. This was not a negotiating matter. If you weren't cool with bowing down and worshipping once the music started things would get very hot for you because you would be thrown into a fiery furnace. If you weren't ok with what had come out of that furnace you would have to be ok with going into that furnace.

So the day came and the horns and the harps and all the other instruments started playing and all the people bowed down and worshipped. That is, all except for three guys who could maybe dress like a Babylonian and talk like a Babylonian but they simply could not worship false gods like a Babylonian.

Immediately they were taken to the king to explain their disobedience. (If you can, take the time and read this story and this whole dialogue in Daniel 3, it's worth it.). The furious king asked them if it was really true that they were stupid enough to refuse to worship his gods and bow before the idol. And before they could answer he continued by saying that he'd give them another chance but if they didn't bow down this time then they'd be thrown into the fiery furnace. *"Then what God will be able to rescue you from my hand?"* he said.

Their response is the whole reason we're looking at this story because it demonstrates such an incredible level of faith that can teach us so much. Imagine what it must have been like to hear them say:

"O Nebuchadnezzar, we do not need to defend ourselves before you in this matter. If we are thrown into the blazing furnace, the God we serve is able to save us from it, and he will rescue us from your hand, O king. But even if he does not, we want you to know, O king, that we will not serve your gods or worship the image of gold you have set up." (Daniel 3:16–18)

These guys had real, genuine, fire-proof faith in God. That's what faith is. It's *"being sure of what we hope for and certain of what we do not see"* (Hebrews 11:1). And though these guys couldn't see exactly how this situation was about to pan out they had faith that God would still be God through it all.

For what it's worth, they were thrown into the fire. The guys who tossed them in were even burnt up and died on the spot. But our three faithful fellows? They were walking around in there with Jesus and eventually walked out and had the king declare that their God was the only true God. No kidding!

None of this would have been possible without faith. For you to be in relationship with God you have to believe He exists. For that relationship to work you have to believe He is who He says He is. And for your life in Him to become all He wants it to be you have to believe that He can do what He says He can do.

If you can have faith in God to forgive your sins and make you new, doesn't that make it easier to believe He can do even more?

What does it mean to YOU to have faith in God? What do you need to trust Him with or believe Him for in your life?

_____

_____

_____

_____

Read Hebrews 11:6. In your own words, why is faith so important and essential to pleasing God?

_____

_____

_____

Today, take the few seconds it'll take you to do this and memorize 2 Corinthians 5:7 and think about what that means for your life.

CHAPTER 23

THIS MEANS WAR!

Can you imagine if you were to go over to the Middle East some day and walk down the street with an "I love the U.S.A." shirt how that would go over in some places? You could go strolling down the street whistling as you go, but in a number of places you're going to find that your shirt and that message is going to get you into a world of hurt.

Why? Because those people are at war against the U.S. and what it stands for. But you already know that. That's why you wouldn't go strolling down some road by a terrorist and scream out "U.S.A." When you realize there's a war going on you behave differently and if you're wise you're going to prepare for inevitable battles.

For you to walk into the middle of a battlefield without any weapon in your hand would be pretty...well...stupid. Now let me be crystal clear with you here: for you to walk through your life having said "yes" to the life that God has offered you and "no" to the slavery of sin and to not be prepared for spiritual attacks is equally as stupid. When you make the decision to follow Christ you need to know that you are guaranteed eternal life and that He will be with you always, but you are not guaranteed some easy, breezy life. It sure would be nice if it did work out that way, though!

Instead you'll soon realize that life is still tough and maybe it even gets tougher for you. That's an honest piece of truth that I have to admit I'm not thrilled to say because some people may think, "Well then why do this whole following Jesus thing if it may make my life even harder?!" Secretly I think we wish that following God would somehow cause us to get out of having to deal with the challenges of life. However, God never said that in following Him we'd not have to deal with the spiritual battles. He just said that in following Him He'd now be on our side watching over us and protecting us.

See, we don't have time here for all the background story, but you should know a few things. When God created man He created them in His image:

So God created man in his own image,
in the image of God he created him;
male and female he created them. (Genesis 1:27)

But before man was ever created there was a moment in the history of heaven where one of the angels decided that he was as important and worthy of praise as God Himself. Crazy right?! So he tried stirring things up and convinced some other angels to rebel against God and God had them cast out of heaven for all eternity and sent to a place of torment for what they'd done. That place was hell. And that rebellious angel was Satan.

How do we fit in? Well, we were created in the image of God. We were unlike any other thing that God created. He made us to be, in a sense, like Him and to have a unique and meaningful and eternal relationship with Him. But that puts a target on our backs from the start because the enemy can't look at us and not see the image of God. It's all over us. So he's out to steal, kill, and destroy us (see John 10:10) any chance he can get. Fortunately, he's no match for God. So we don't need to be worried that we're on the losing side. God's promised those who follow Him life abundantly (Seriously, go check out John 10:10!). And that means that no matter what battles we face the war is ultimately already won.

I want to close out this chapter by giving you a little boot camp training for the spiritual warfare that you'll eventually face in life. If you've ever watched one of those nature shows where you see those male moose battle for dominance you know what a head-butt is really all about! They come barreling at each other full speed and then put their heads down so their massive antlers go crashing into the antlers of the opposing male. They're fighting for turf. The one who wins is the one whose antlers are larger and tougher, and whose bodies are bigger and stronger.

And so when you think about it, the battle is really won before the heads ever collide. It's in the preparation in the spring and summer with what they choose to eat and do that determines the winner in the fall.

So prepare now. Eat up God's word and develop a healthy, robust relationship with Him. It may simply seem like a nice way of making life great right now, but later on it may be what helps you make it through when the battles of life come your way.

. . . .

Take a minute and read Ephesians 6:10–13.

What schemes or attacks have you seen the devil try to use against you personally?

_____

_____

_____

_____

_____

_____

_____

_____

Sometimes we have to remind ourselves that we're not battling the forces we can see but our ultimate enemy who we can't see. Why do you think it's hard to remember this?

_____

_____

_____

_____

What does it mean to you to know that God is with you giving you the strength during these battles?

_____

_____

_____

_____

_____

_____

CHAPTER 24

FOLLOW THE RULES

There is a foundational, ground-level, basic, absolutely essential thing that you need to understand about what we believe as followers of Christ. And that truth is this: God wants what's best for you. He really does! More than you even want what's best for you. Really. Let me show you how that's true.

See, we think we want what's best for us. We have this idea of how our life should go, what we should get, what shouldn't happen to us, and who should do what in our lives. You know it's true because when things don't go a certain way, when you don't get what you feel you should've gotten, when things happen that you feel never should have, and when people let you down you get pretty upset, don't you?

Now here's the problem, have you ever looked back on something that you thought was bad at first, but then realized that it actually was for good? We don't always get to see the full picture when we're in the moment, but we sometimes see things a lot differently once the moment has passed and we can look back. I know I've had plenty of times in my life where I saw things differently than when I did in the moment. So in the moment you don't always know what's going to be best for you.

That's the difference between you and God. He sees it all and you and I don't. So what happens is that when you look at the Bible, both in the Old Testament, black-and-white commands as well as in the guide to Christian living that's given in the New Testament you can be tempted to see this: RULES RULES RULES. That's the way some people view this whole "Christian thing." They think it's all about rules we have to follow and a God who apparently just wants to limit our lives by killing our fun.

The truth of the matter is that if God didn't love us then He wouldn't tell us what to do. But God sees the big picture and He sees what's *really* best for us and not just what we think is best for us. There's even a poem in the Old Testament where God is telling His people to realize the difference in the way we may view a situation and the way God views it. Check it out:

"For my thoughts are not your thoughts,
neither are your ways my ways,"
declares the Lord.
"As the heavens are higher than the earth,
so are my ways higher than your ways
and my thoughts than your thoughts." (Isaiah 55:8–9)

So God gives us instruction through His word and, as we've talked about before, He gives us His Holy Spirit to give us that sort of "gut check" because He wants us to know when something is right and is best for us and when something is wrong and going to hurt us. After that it comes down to the decision we have to make. Are we going to allow ourselves to believe that we know better than God?

That was the original temptation back in the very beginning with Adam and Eve. They were tempted to disobey God and eat fruit they were directly told not to eat. So why did they? They thought they knew better than God. They thought He was holding out on them.

You'll face moments like that too. Ok, maybe not with fruit from some forbidden tree. For you it may be that you're tempted to tell some small lie that will make life a little easier for you...or so you think. It may be that you're tempted to gossip about somebody and say some things that need to be said...or so you think. It can be you want to think that, do that, or say that all because you believe that "that" will be best for you. But God has your best interest in mind and so if you love Him and really want what's best for you, you'll follow His instruction and do what

He says to do and not do what He says not to do. When you do that it pleases God and it protects you from a world of pain and trouble.

One final thought before we close this out. The direction this all happens is so crucial. Some people get it all turned around and end up thinking it's all about them. They look at it like this: I do the right thing --> because there are rules to follow --> to get God to love me. And that's what a lot of people think it looks like to be a Christian and think that it's up to them to be good enough people. So they work really hard to avoid sin and do what's right to earn God's love. It doesn't work that way!

It actually works like this: God loves me as I am and wants what's best for me --> so He gives me rules to follow --> and so in response to His love I love Him back by following those instructions. And because God knows what's best, your best life will be found when you listen to what He has to say.

. . . .

We all tend to have a bit of a "rebel" in us that wants to break any rules we're given. Why do you think that is?

We spent a lot of time talking here about how God loves us. Why does that matter when it comes to the instructions He gives us in the Bible?

_____

_____

_____

_____

_____

Read Matthew 26:41. Looking at that verse, what do you think your main challenge in obedience is going to be? And how can you prepare to win that challenge?

_____

_____

_____

_____

_____

_____

CHAPTER 25

MIND YOUR THOUGHTS

So I have an honest confession to make here. I'm not really all that into sports. Growing up I never was and am just now slowly getting into watching them. For what it's worth, I did play soccer (the best sport there is to play) from kindergarten to ninth grade. And I did go to my high school's football games, though that was mostly depressing because we didn't exactly have the best record.

Have you ever watched a sports team get ready to play a big game? It's something pretty cool to see. They get out on the field and stretch and get their bodies ready to play. But then they do something that's just about as important, if you ask me. Once they're done stretching and their bodies are ready, they get their heads in the game. Ever heard that saying? They start circling up and yelling about how they're there to win. Win! Win!!! They're jumping. They're pushing each other to get the blood pumping for their teammates. All this yelling, pushing, and chanting is all because they realize something very important: Your thoughts affect the results, so think right!

It reminds me of a quote that always gets me thinking:

"Watch your thoughts, they become words.
Watch your words, they become actions.
Watch your actions, they become habits.
Watch your habits, they become your character.
Watch your character, it becomes your destiny."

There is this progression that's at work behind the scenes of our lives whether we realize it or not. In those game moments the coaches and the players realize that if they want to have a chance at winning this game that they're about to play then they need to get their minds prepped and warmed up to win. What we think about does eventually come out as our words and eventually our actions. There are many people who walk through life thinking that their thoughts and feelings are just there because of what's happened to them. For those people, they don't control their thoughts; their thoughts control them. But there's another way.

Paul, one of the guys that God used to write a lot of the New Testament of the Bible, had a kind of rough story. He had been on top of his career and life path as a Jewish leader. But he was one of those guys who went a 110% in whatever he did and he was determined to end this whole Christian movement. So he would go around from city to city finding where they were and then arresting them and even being a part of putting them to death.

It wasn't until one day when God knocked him to the ground, blinded him, and spoke to him audibly that he was persecuting God Himself that Paul finally came to know God personally. Yes, he got his sight back a couple of days later. But the rest of Paul's life is littered with moments where he's able to tell people about God and then moments where doing that lands him in prison, gets him nearly killed, and has him disliked by many. Paul knew a lot about rough circumstances. That's what makes it even cooler that God used him write this to His church.

Finally, brothers, whatever is true, whatever is noble, whatever is right, whatever is pure, whatever is lovely, whatever is admirable—if anything is excellent or praiseworthy—think about such things. (Philippians 4:8)

"Think about such things." If he tells us what to think about it means we can control what we think about. That means that Paul could've been depressed, convinced that it was all worthless, and decided to focus on all the wrong things going on, but he chose to own his thoughts. And that's what we need to do. They're our thoughts and so we need to own them.

The enemy will try to use your thoughts to destroy you. He'll try to convince you you're not good enough. You can own your thoughts and remind yourself that it's not about you being good enough, it's about God being good. He'll try to convince you that you should give up when it gets tough. You can own your thoughts and remind yourself that God will never leave you and that you can and should persevere. He'll try to use your thoughts to convince you to justify doing something wrong. But you can own your thoughts and remind yourself that God has given you a way out of any temptation and that your best life is found in obedience to God.

I've found that all real lasting change in your life will begin with a change of thought. So if you want to do your part in constantly making your life better, make your thoughts better. And be aware that that's the battlefield that you will most have to fight the enemy on. So mind your thoughts!

. . . .

Looking at Philippians 4:8, which we already read in this chapter, which of the list of things that we're supposed to think about is the biggest challenge for you? Why?

_____

_____

_____

_____

_____

_____

_____

Go take a look at Romans 12:2. We're told not to conform to the pattern of this world. What patterns do you see in this world?

_____

_____

_____

_____

Now that verse also says that, rather than conforming, we should be transformed by the renewing of our minds. What old thoughts of yours may need thrown out in that renewing process? What new ones may have to come in?

_____

_____

_____

_____

_____

_____

CHAPTER 26

HANDLING THE DOUBTS

We just talked in the last chapter about owning our thoughts and I want to take a whole chapter to deal with a topic that you'll eventually face. When some people face it it ends up taking them out of the whole game. They decide they can't fight it and choose to just give in. But it is something you can win against and it can even help make you a stronger believer. What am I talking about? Doubts. Yes, doubts.

Let's take a second to look at a story that shows us how we should handle our doubts. We're going to read the whole story because it's so worth it to get the full picture.

When they came to the other disciples, they saw a large crowd around them and the teachers of the law arguing with them. As soon as all the people saw Jesus, they were overwhelmed with wonder and ran to greet him.
"What are you arguing with them about?" he asked.
A man in the crowd answered, "Teacher, I brought you my son, who is possessed by a spirit that has robbed him of speech. Whenever it seizes him, it throws him to the ground. He foams at the mouth, gnashes his teeth and becomes rigid. I asked your disciples to drive out the spirit, but they could not." "O unbelieving generation," Jesus replied, "how long shall I stay with you? How long shall I put up with you? Bring the boy to me."
So they brought him. When the spirit saw Jesus, it immediately threw the boy into a convulsion. He fell to the ground and rolled around, foaming at the mouth.
Jesus asked the boy's father, "How long has he been like this?"
"From childhood," he answered. "It has often thrown him into fire or

water to kill him. But if you can do anything, take pity on us and help us."

" 'If you can'?" said Jesus. "Everything is possible for him who believes." Immediately the boy's father exclaimed, "I do believe; help me overcome my unbelief!"

When Jesus saw that a crowd was running to the scene, he rebuked the evil spirit. "You deaf and mute spirit," he said, "I command you, come out of him and never enter him again."

The spirit shrieked, convulsed him violently and came out. The boy looked so much like a corpse that many said, "He's dead." But Jesus took him by the hand and lifted him to his feet, and he stood up. (Mark 9:14–27)

See, this man's immediate crisis was that his son was demon-possessed and was being thrown into fire and water to try to kill him. Jesus wants to deal with that. But He also wants to deal with the other issue here: the father's doubt. After all, the father did say to Jesus that he wanted Him to heal his son *"if he could."* And Jesus calls him out on his lack of belief. Then He assures the dad that everything is possible for those who believe. The man's response speaks so much to me: *"I do believe; help me overcome my unbelief."*

First off, he acknowledges his doubt. He says he believes but he also recognizes there are areas where he still has questions and struggles to believe. After years of working in ministry, I have to admit that I still have those moments too. I sometimes struggle to understand everything and buy it all. If you are just playing games and want to be a Christian because you think it's what you should do, then you may not have many doubts. But I think that if you're really giving God your life and you're "all in" then you're going to have questions and you'll have moments when you doubt. That's not terrible!

What you do with your doubts is crucial. It's not enough to recognize that you have doubt. Great. But the father in this story goes to Jesus and says, "Help me with this doubt." He doesn't just accept it and say that it's just the way life is going to be for him. He wants to find a solution to his lingering doubt and so he goes to Jesus looking for help.

I'll be honest, I think it's just plain lazy how some people deal with their doubts. I've talked to too many people who say they'd like to believe in "that whole God thing" but they just have doubts. The problem is that I often find that they don't really want to believe. In fact, they're totally ok with living for themselves. They may have questions that make it hard to believe but when you really want to know the truth you go looking for it. And while I've personally had tough questions I've had to wrestle with, I ask God to help me and I look into finding the answer. And you know what I've found? God isn't intimidated by our questions. He realizes that He's God and that means He's beyond our range of fully understanding. Maybe it would help us to realize that fact and be willing to go to Him with our doubts and say, "I do believe; help me overcome my unbelief!"

· ·

What are some of the questions you have at this point? What are some of the things you're struggling to understand?

_____

_____

_____

_____

_____

_____

_____

_____

Who do you have in your life that is spiritually mature enough that you can talk to about some of these questions you have? I challenge you to actually find a time in the next few days to ask them some of your questions to see if maybe they can help you out.

_____

_____

_____

_____

_____

_____

Take a minute here and just pray and talk to God about these questions you have. Be honest. He can handle it.

CHAPTER 27

NOT ASHAMED

I'm not proud of this. Seriously, you need to know that right off the bat or you'll think I'm ok with the fact that I was kind of a jerk, but when I was in middle school I was embarrassed to have my younger brother with me at times. See, I thought I was cool stuff. If you'd seen me then you'd know I couldn't have been more misguided. But I was trying! And I was afraid that my brother was going to ruin that for me. So I would avoid him at times and act like he wasn't there so people wouldn't potentially judge me based off of him. For what it's worth, much time has passed since then and that brother and I are very close now. He can still embarrass me every once in a while but it's all intentional now!

It amazes me what we people will do to maintain our image. I've seen people dress a certain way, talk a certain way, like certain things, and decide to dislike certain things all to seem "cool." And of course then there are all those people who "couldn't care less what people think" of them. It's kind of funny how much people who don't care what I think of them will make a real effort to make sure I know that they don't care... almost as if they do actually care what I think.

I've even seen people play down their relationship with God or deny it all together just to seem cool. Let's be honest, giving your life to a God you can't see, following the example of His Son who lived two thousand years ago, listening to His Spirit which you can't exactly put your finger on, choosing to sacrifice your desires for the needs of those who can do nothing for you, and saying "no" to the selfish desires that so many people are living by seems kind of...well...uncool. Dropping the name of "Jesus" in a rap song may be cool here and there, but actually living for Him is the kind of radical thing that can sometimes leave you on the outside of the "in" crowd. It almost certainly will make you stand out.

It's for that reason that our friend Paul encouraged believers in Rome with this:

I am not ashamed of the gospel, because it is the power of God for the salvation of everyone who believes: first for the Jew, then for the Gentile. For in the gospel a righteousness from God is revealed, a righteousness that is by faith from first to last, just as it is written: "The righteous will live by faith." (Romans 1:16–17)

See, in Rome it wasn't just a matter of cool or uncool, popular or unpopular. It was a matter of life or death for some of them. They were beginning to face persecution and abuse for this gospel that we've been talking about. And it's that gospel — the good news — that Paul knew was worth being unashamed.

It may make sense to be ashamed of the fact that you sing in the shower, or that you can quote every Star Wars movie, or that you have lucky socks that you never wash, or that you like boy bands. There's plenty we could — and probably should! — be embarrassed about, but when something has the power of God for the salvation of everyone who believes then it really makes no sense to be ashamed of that.

It won't always be a popular message. But it's not about popularity, it's about power. The gospel has power to set people free who are being held captive by their sin. It has the power to give hope to those who are convinced there's nothing worth hoping for. It has the power to bring life to people who feel dead. It flies in the face of the way this world works. It challenges the standards that make so many people tick. Just look at the stories of Jesus and what He would say and do. He rocked His world with a message that was both life-giving as well as incredibly backwards from the way so many were living.

This message of hope, love, joy, peace, and eternal life was worth it to Jesus so much that He died proclaiming it. There's a really good chance,

I would imagine, that you won't ever have to die because of the gospel you believe and follow. But there will be times when you'll be tempted to back away and be ashamed of your faith because it will cost you. Maybe it'll cost you a friendship, a relationship, or an opportunity to just blend in. Maybe you'll get picked on for what you choose to believe. But let me challenge you: Jesus was willing to die to give you this good news. Can't you be willing to live your life for Him rather than the opinions of others?

· ·

What has the gospel (the good news of Jesus and what He's done to restore your relationship with God) meant for you personally?

_____

_____

_____

_____

"The righteous will live by faith," said that passage in Romans we read earlier. Why do you think faith is so important in being unashamed?

_____

_____

_____

_____

Take a minute and write down a personal message from you to God telling Him why you will choose to not be ashamed of the gospel.

_____

_____

_____

CHAPTER 28

SPREAD THE WORD

Have you ever seen something so funny that you just knew you needed to tell a friend about it? Or, if you could actually do it, show them so they could see it too? Have you ever had something wild happen to you that just had to tell someone about because they just needed to know? Have you ever had a tragedy happen in your life that you just wanted to talk over with someone close to you? I'm willing to bet you said "yes" to each of those questions. You know why? Because when big things happen in our life we want to share them with others.

One day about two thousand years ago a certain woman had a pretty big thing happen in her life too. We don't know her name but we do know a bit about her and her sins because it came up in a conversation she had with Jesus that was recorded in the book of John in the Bible. Yep, the conversation started kind of simple enough that day but then eventually came to Jesus asking her some real tough and honest questions. Then, after fighting back a bit, she realized that she was in the presence of God and that He was reaching out to her. So she responded and found healing for her broken life. But the story gets even better. Just like I said about earlier, look at what she does:

Then, leaving her water jar, the woman went back to the town and said to the people, "Come, see a man who told me everything I ever did. Could this be the Christ?" They came out of the town and made their way toward him.
Many of the Samaritans from that town believed in him because of the woman's testimony, "He told me everything I ever did." So when the Samaritans came to him, they urged him to stay with them, and he stayed two days. And because of his words many more became believers.

They said to the woman, "We no longer believe just because of what you said; now we have heard for ourselves, and we know that this man really is the Savior of the world." (John 4:28–30, 39–42)

Her life had been changed and she wasn't going to just sit back and think about what it meant for her. She wanted to tell people about it and give them a chance to experience the life change that she had just had. She was contagious, in a good way! And that's how it should be.

My assumption is that if you're reading this you've probably recently experienced the amazing life-changing power of Jesus Christ and His forgiveness. Giving your life to Him really is the best life decision you could EVER make. Without giving our lives over to God we have to carry the weight of our past sins ourselves, try to make the most of this present life as we can, and, honestly, we are destined for a future in hell separated from God. Not good! But when you accept God's forgiveness and give your life to Him it means your past is forgiven. It means you can have a meaningful life here in the present. And it means that you have a hope for a future shared with Him in heaven. So that's why it's such a big deal that you've made this decision. And that's why it's so important for you to share this good news with others.

I realize that can be a bit intimidating for some people. Maybe you're shy. Maybe you don't know what to say. Maybe you're afraid. Here are some simple things to keep in mind that should help you to see how sharing your faith is something that is really do-able for you!

Share your story. The woman didn't get up and preach. She didn't have to have all the answers to all the questions. She just went out and told people what Jesus had done in her life. And so for you, it's as simple as that. What has Jesus done for you? Doesn't matter if it seems to be a small thing. It probably isn't. And even still, tell someone!

Think long-term. Our souls are eternal and every person you meet

IT ALL STARTS HERE

will live for eternity either in heaven or in hell. It's pretty heavy stuff, I realize. So allow that to help motivate you past any fear you may have in sharing with someone the key to eternal life.

Write down your story. I've found it really helps you to feel more confident in sharing it when you've taken some time to write it down beforehand. Start off with what your life was before. And then talk about how you came to that point where you decided to follow Jesus. And then share as much as you can about how your life is different now.

Don't give up. Following Christ doesn't make your life perfect. We still go through tough times. We still face disappointment, hurt and questions. The good thing is that we have the Holy Spirit with us through all of that. And so just realize that you may be disappointed when a friend isn't interested in Christ. Don't give up. Just keep sharing, because eventually you'll get to be a part of someone else's story of how they came to know Jesus!

. . . .

Who do you know that you can and should share Jesus with?

_____

_____

_____

_____

_____

_____

Write out the outline of your story here. You can write it out in more detail somewhere else if you'd like.

_____

_____

_____

_____

_____

_____

So you have the names of people you're going to talk to and you have your story written out. Take a minute and write out a prayer asking God to give you what you think you're going to need to do this (for example: the words, the courage, the opportunity, etc.).

_____

_____

_____

_____

_____

_____

CHAPTER 29

WHAT ABOUT WHEN I STILL MESS UP?

As we end the near of this book I'd like to shoot straight with you about something important. You're going to mess up. You're going to sin. You're going to know something is wrong and you're going to do it anyway. And there will be times that you'll know you should do something and you're going to decide not to. I'm sure of it. Why? Because when you become a Christian you become a new creation (remember that?) but you do not become perfect this side of eternity. You will still have a sinful nature that will battle against you and there will be plenty of times you'll win. But then there will be other times that, instead, you sin.

I always learn better with stories, so allow me to share another one with you from the Bible. You can read it for yourself in Matthew chapters 26 & 27. At this point in the life of Jesus it was getting to be the time where He would make His way to the cross to die for our sins. He knew that, but none of His twelve disciples who had been going everywhere with Him for the last three years knew where He was going next.

You may have heard of Judas before. Well, even though he was one of Jesus' disciples he decided that Jesus was not doing things the way he wanted them to be done and so he agreed to betray Jesus for thirty pieces of silver. He basically sold Jesus like a slave to the religious leaders of that time who wanted to see Him killed. The same night that Judas would leave the group to get the soldiers to arrest Him, Jesus was eating a meal with all twelve of His disciples. And at one point He essentially called Judas out for what he was going to do. But that's not the only guy He called out that night. He also pointed the finger at Peter and said that he was going to deny Him three times before the next morning came. Pretty crazy dinner, right?

Just like Jesus said would happen, Judas brought a troop of guards from the temple to arrest Him that night. And just like Jesus said would happen, Peter ended up denying that he knew Jesus three times before the rooster crowed to announce that morning had come. Both of these guys messed up BIG TIME! Their mistakes made history and people have been talking about them and learning from them for hundreds upon hundreds of years. But they were really just people. And people mess up. And that's how I know that you'll mess up. Truth is, we all mess up. But what we do when we mess up separates those who will go the distance in their relationship with God from those who will get knocked out by their sin.

I didn't finish the story earlier so let me get back to it. See, Jesus ended up going to trial, even though it was an unfair one, and was sentenced to death. As I imagine you already know, Jesus was hung on a cross and He died (Don't forget Matthew chapter 28 tells us He beat death and rose from the dead!). But the guilt of all of this was too much for Judas. He realized what He'd done and decided he couldn't go on any longer. He actually hanged himself. For Judas, his failure was final. But it doesn't have to be that way!

Failure does not need to be final. Instead it can be an opportunity for you and I to learn, to grow closer to God, and to improve. Peter figured this out. He was heartbroken after denying Jesus. You can imagine what it must have felt like for him to know he'd abandoned his friend in His greatest time of need. But when you read the story in John 21 you see that Jesus was looking to forgive Peter and restore him after this big mess up. He had a second chance!

The difference between these two men was that Judas carried his guilt to his death and Peter offered his guilt to God to give him life. My friend, you cannot bear the weight of your own sin. We never could. That's why back in the Old Testament they would do all those animal sacrifices, because the penalty of sin is death (Romans 6:23). Sin is serious business and it breaks the heart of God and distances us from Him. But we don't have to wallow in our sin like a pig wallows in the mud. There's a way out. Jesus died on that cross we just talked about so that you and I wouldn't have to pay the price for our sins. He paid it! Ultimately, He died so that we could live.

He didn't die so that you could feel guilty and beat yourself up for the mistakes you've made or the ones you're going to make along the way. He already paid for them. So use that rope of your mistakes and, rather than hanging yourself with it and calling it quits, throw it out of the pit you've gotten into and ask for God to rescue you. When you're honest with God about your sins, when you repent and turn from them, and when you come running to Him for help, He's more than willing to pick you up, brush you off, and continue walking along with you.

. . . .

Go read John 3:16–17. In case you don't know, condemning means to express public disproval and dislike. Let's say that God was interested in condemning you, what could He blame you for specifically?

_____

_____

_____

_____

What does it mean for you personally that God isn't interested in condemning you but in setting you free from sin?

_____

_____

_____

_____

_____

Think about it for a minute. Why do you think it's sometimes difficult to go to God when you make mistakes?

_____

_____

_____

_____

_____

Take a moment and thank God in your own words for loving you enough to forgive you when you sin.

CHAPTER 30

UNBURIED TREASURE

He handed you the money and then handed some money to the two friends you were with and with a few words he was gone. And so there you stood with a hand full of cash and a head full of confusion. You'd known him for some time but you had never had this happen before where he just handed you a wad of cash like this. You looked at your friends and they looked just as confused. The only thing he'd said was that he would be back. Did he expect you to buy something for him? Did he want you just to hold onto it for him? Or did he want you to invest it somehow? How should you know?

There was a story like this one that Jesus once told His disciples when He was teaching them one day (See Matthew 25:14–29). It was an important lesson about what we do with what God's given us. So let me jump back to the story.

See, the one who had been given the most went out and invested it and was able to double his money. And actually the other one who had been given a little less was still able to double that money he'd been given by investing it. But the third one who had been given the least was so afraid of messing things up that he just buried the money. He didn't know what to do with it. It was so little in his eyes that he didn't want to bother with it. When the man came back for his money he was very pleased with the two who'd taken and done something with their money, but he was furious at the one who just buried his gift.

What a shame to have been given a gift and to not use it at all but to just bury it! Jesus' point is pretty clear: God has given each one of us something that we can use for Him and His glory. It looks different for each of us. Some are gifted talkers, others are great listeners, some have artistic gifts, some have athletic gifts, some are good thinkers, some are good doers, some are good at math, some are good at cooking, some are gifted with money, some are good with people, some are good with tools, some are gifted at a certain instrument, some can sing, some are gifted at being extra kind to others, some are gifted writers, and some are good at cheering people up. And truthfully I could go on and on.

There are so many gifts we can have. And somewhere in that list are gifts that you've been given. You may be thinking, "No, not really!" because you're not the best at it or you know someone who's better. But without a doubt I can say that you have been given SOMETHING that you can do. Remember, the one guy thought that his gift was so small that he didn't even do anything with it. We can often be tempted to think that because we're not "all that great" that we shouldn't do anything with the gifts we've been given.

One of my absolute favorite verses in the Bible tells us how we were created by God who cared enough to give us each a unique set of things that we could do. Check it out:

For we are God's masterpiece. He has created us anew in Christ Jesus, so we can do the good things he planned for us long ago. (Ephesians 2:10, NLT)

Catch that? You are God's masterpiece. It may not feel like that all the time. I get that! But regardless of our feelings God has made us special and unique and given us special and unique gifts and opportunities for us to do something good in this world. How cool is that?! The question is whether we do something with them or not.

And let's be honest. Your gifts aren't really for you anyway. Seriously. Your gifts are things God has given you so that you can give them away and use them for something bigger than yourself. We all know the world has problems and issues. Nearly everyone can see the problems, but only special people can do something to provide solutions. God has called His Church to be the hope of the world and to work to make it right. And you know what's cool? He's given you something that you can do to be a part of that. So go for it! It doesn't matter how "wonderful" you are. It only matters how willing you are.

. . . .

Alright, with all this gift talk it's time to get you thinking. What gifts do you think you may have? List as many as you can!

_____

_____

_____

_____

How does the fact that God has given you any gifts at all show His love for you and the plans He has for you?

_____

_____

_____

_____

What do you think God may be calling you to do with the gifts He's given? Be as specific as you can.

_____

_____

_____

_____

_____

CHAPTER 31

JESUS, TAKE THE WHEEL?

There's this little joke that I like to say when I try to be funny. It goes something like this: I've decided how I want to die. I want to go out like my grandfather did — peacefully and in his sleep. And I definitely know that I do NOT want to go out like the rest of the people in his car did that day!

For the record, no, that's not how either of my grandfathers passed away. It's simply a joke, but it's one that I find pretty funny.

As we end this book together it's a bit of a contradiction. We're coming to the end of our trip but, like I said at the very beginning this book, this whole thing is just the beginning. Life is a journey and our life in Christ is one that will begin here on earth when we make the decision to follow Him and it will continue throughout all eternity as we join Him in heaven in the place He's prepared for those who believe. We've got a lot to look forward to! But we're not there yet, and our journey starts now.

When I was a little kid I remember going on road trips with my family. One of my favorite memories of those trips was something my dad would do that maybe your dad or mom did with you too. He would put me on his lap and he would let me drive! Ok, so I wasn't really driving, but I got to steer a little. Of course my dad was pushing the gas and break pedals when needed and he had his hands on the steering wheel just in case I had the wonderful idea of pulling hard to one side or the other. In the same way, our heavenly Father is looking for us to let Him drive.

I've tried to get this message across a couple of times now and let me say it again. Being a Christian is not just about having a name tag that says you prayed a prayer or made a decision once a while back. It's about having a living, active relationship with Jesus Christ and allowing Him to be your best friend and Lord. "Lord" — there's a word we don't hear too often in regular conversation. You'll find it used quite a bit in the Bible when they talk about Jesus, but what does it mean? Let me tell you. Back in Jesus' day when someone was "lord" that means they were the boss. They called the shots. And so when Jesus is referred to as "Lord of lords" it's basically saying He's the boss of bosses, the president of presidents. Jesus runs this show.

Ultimately God IS in control. But He's also given us free will so we can choose whether we will love Him and live our lives for Him. You get to choose whether you will make Jesus lord in your life. No one else can make that choice for you. And that's the beauty of this, that you get to freely love God. You're not a robot forced to worship Him and follow His lead. You're a living, breathing human being with the freedom to *choose* to worship Him and follow His lead.

The challenge is this: we like being in control of our own lives. I know some people can be what we call a "control freak" but I think we're all a bunch of control freaks to a certain extent. We don't really like people telling us what to do. We like to figure things out for ourselves and make our own decisions. Haven't you given a friend advice because you've been there and done that and they just ignore you because they need to find out for themselves? See? We naturally want to find things out for ourselves, trust ourselves, and do what seems right to ourselves.

One of my favorite passages of Scripture addresses this issue and tells us a lot about what it means to make Jesus Lord over our lives:

Trust in the Lord with all your heart
        and lean not on your own understanding;
in all your ways acknowledge him,
        and he will make your paths straight. (Proverbs 3:5–6)

We're all on this journey called life. You and I jumped into it midway, and honestly we're mostly trying to figure it out as we go because no one seems to have found the pause button. But life continues and the only secret to figuring it out is in getting to know the One who created life itself. God has always existed and will always exist. He's beyond what we'll ever fully understand because He's God. That can cause us to question and doubt, but He can be trusted. He loved us enough to send His Son Jesus Christ to die on cross so that we could be freed from our sin and have new life in Him.

In that new life it only works if we give over control. Sure, you may be sitting on His lap with your hands on the wheel but you'd better let Him drive and call the shots! His plan for your life is better than you could ever imagine. Trust Him with all your heart. Realize your feelings are fickle and can't be trusted like He can be. In your everyday life be aware that He's there with you, watching you, and wanting your very best. When you let Him drive your life He'll take you for the ride of your life. Sure, there will be bumps and it won't always be easy, but you were made by Him and for Him so trust Him and let Him write a great story with your life!

Let me end with one of my favorite quotes to challenge you with:

The world has yet to see what God can do with and for and through and in and by the man who is fully and wholly consecrated to Him. I will try my utmost to be that man. - D.L. Moody

IT ALL STARTS HERE

If you were honest, what parts of your life do you think will be the most challenging to surrender to God?

_____

_____

_____

_____

_____

Knowing that God is who He is and you are who you are, in your own words talk about why it makes sense in your life for Him to be the one running the show?

_____

_____

_____

_____

_____

_____

_____

I've mentioned the writer of much of the New Testament, Paul, a couple of times in this book. Well, in the letter he wrote to the people of the church in Philippi he said this:

"Therefore, my dear friends, as you have always obeyed—not only in my presence, but now much more in my absence—continue to work out your salvation with fear and trembling, for it is God who works in you to will and to act according to his good purpose" (Phillippians 2:12b–13).

He had left them and wanted to know that they weren't going to quit or coast but that they would continue. Continue to work out their salvation. This means that they would continue to learn, to listen, to love, to look for what God's doing, and to live their lives totally for Him. He knew it was easier when they had him there helping. And he knew it would be a bit more of a challenge when he was gone.

In a similar way, now that this book is done I realize it may be a bit more of a challenge for you to continue going. But you have the written Word of God. You've got a God who loves you and has made His Holy Spirit available to work in you. And I'm betting you have people who are cheering you on as you go. So go! God's not done with you. In fact, He's just started. Now it's time to see where this goes!